Herkimer County
Community College Library
Herkimer, New York
13350

Our Daughter Learns to Read and Write

A case study from birth to three

Marcia Baghban
West Virginia College of Graduate Studies

International Reading Association
800 Barksdale Road, Box 8139
Newark, Delaware 19714

Copyright 1984 by the
International Reading Association, Inc.

Library of Congress Cataloging in Publication Data

Baghban, Marcia, 1942-
   Our daughter learns to read and write.

   Bibliography: p.
   1. Language acquisition.   2. Language arts (Preschool)
I. Title.
P118.B25   1984   401'.9   84-10868
ISBN 0-87207-956-2

Contents

LIST OF FIGURES FOR SAMPLES OF WRITTEN LANGUAGE

Foreword

It was an exciting time. Carolyn Burke, Virginia Woodward, and I had just launched our studies of what children 3, 4, 5, and 6 years old know about literacy and literacy learning prior to coming to school.

Some members of the profession questioned our sanity. Everyone "knew" that advanced forms of literacy, like reading and writing, were built from and upon an oral language base. Everyone "knew" that while oral language was acquired naturally, reading and writing must be taught. Everyone "knew" that reading and writing required some executive monitoring function which cognitively was beyond the developmental level of children this age.

But, it was a new age. An age which was saying that theories of literacy ought to do more than explain a convenient subset of only some language learners' behaviors. An age which was speculating that maybe, just maybe, theories of literacy learning which can't explain all of the behaviors of at least one language learner aren't viable theories at all. An age which was demanding that theories of literacy and literacy learning be rooted in what real language learners were really doing. An age which was calling for theories of language use or practical theory. An age which was suggesting that what we thought we knew was best not considered sacred. An age which was suggesting that past assumptions about the supremacy of oral language and the unnaturalness of written language learning were in need of questioning and testing.

And we were amazed! Young children knew more about reading and writing than any of us had ever dared imagine. Not only was there literacy before schooling, but we had begun our studies too late.

And then came Marcia Baghban—she wanted to start earlier, from birth! What, pray tell, would the profession's reaction be to studying reading and writing even before three?

In this theoretically noisy era, Marcia and Giti quietly set out. At first, all that seemed to be produced were cute language stories. Only in theoretical perspective did these anecdotes become "data," and, in historical perspective, become a teething ring for rethinking literacy and the basic processes involved in literacy learning.

This book doesn't need a long introduction. Marcia Baghban is such a sensitive observer and writer that she makes Giti speak not only for herself, but for children everywhere. While the Gitis of the world are special, we are finding out they are not unusual.

In pursuit of understanding and making sense of her world, Giti expands and explores the potentials of written language literacy for herself and for others. In so doing, Giti teaches us what the generative potential of literacy is all about.

Giti helps her mother appreciate literacy and her world as much as her mother helps Giti appreciate literacy and her world. Giti teaches us that the roads in and to literacy go both ways.

Giti's written language learning curriculum is not nearly as tidy as is the one we currently plan for children in schools. She mixes her study of literacy with art, story reading, listening, speaking, gesture, dance, and temper tantrum or two. Giti teaches us that there's more than a bit of drama and litter in literacy.

Giti's scope and sequence chart is governed more by those demonstrations available in the context of literacy she encounters than by a preordained order in the systems of language. She demonstrates that participation in a literacy event is its own readiness and that experience, rather than age; is the key to understanding what Giti and other language learners are psycholinguistically and sociolinguistically able to do. In the end, Giti convinces us that what she is engaged in is real literacy, not some pseudo form of literacy.

Reading, writing, and the reasoning these processes make possible are often perceived as solitary discoveries and work. Giti shows us that this work is peopled, and that their quiet presence in both the artifact and form of literacy events makes a significant difference. The true message of Giti's and her mother's story is for us to fill, personally and professionally, the child's environment with not only print, but ourselves.

Jerome C. Harste
Indiana University

Introduction

Learning to Talk

The child is born into the world with the instinct to survive. She notes that her crying gets her a dry diaper, something to ease her stomach, and company in the middle of the night. Even a minimal fulfillment of these basic needs, reinforced by eye contact with caregivers, helps her realize that she is not alone in the world, and that some kind of bridging goes on between her and her caregivers (Bruner, 1978). When most of the sensory-touching events in her daily life are complemented by caregiver questions, explanations, rhymes, stories, and songs, her means to become a member of the world of communicators is assured.

The speech act is self-reinforcing. Once the infant communicates, she wants to communicate more. She learns to differentiate her cries and to wait for responses. She grunts, gurgles, coos, smiles, and points to supplement communication. Through babbling, she establishes a broad picture of how language sounds, and begins to fill in the pieces.

Next, the child labels objects, events, and people in her immediate environment, categorizing her labels syntactically and semantically. To her, cups, saucers, bowls, and the large sink are not only objects but objects that belong in the kitchen. She determines that shoes, shirts, jeans, and jackets are not only items but clothing kept in her closet or worn. She notices the parts needed for the completion of an act. If the caregiver has shoes in hand, the child hunts for socks. She picks up on words and actions that cue. The appearance of her stroller predicts a trip outdoors. She tests hypotheses and retains the strategies and solutions that work for her. While integrating new information with old, she employs her ever-expanding knowledge of the world and her linguistic model as touchstones (Smith, 1975a). She uses language to help her get a handle on her world.

Central to the concept of the speech act is dialogue. While the infant moves toward toddlerhood, the successful caregiver directs her conversation at the child's competence. From the beginning of their relationship, the caregiver assumes the infant understands more than she can verbalize. The caregiver modifies her speech to enhance communication (Snow, 1977), and encourages response from the infant. As the child's competence develops, the caregiver responds to the child as an evolving conversational partner, and begins to hold her responsible for previous knowledge. For example, the caregiver may ask questions with falling or rising intonation, depending on whether she feels the child knows the answer to her question (Pines, 1979). And because the caregiver is concerned with the development of the child's communicative competence, she focuses on the child's understanding of reality. If the child points to a sheep and says, "Dog," the caregiver may correct the truth value of her utterance by saying, "Sheep." She might also provide additional information which would help the child distinguish the two animals in the future. However, the caregiver may not correct the grammar if the child says, "We goed downtown and buyed two mouses," because she has understood the message, and the child would not tune in to this kind of correction because the message has been communicated (Bellugi, 1970).

While the child is maturing, she is simultaneously socialized by the cultural group into which her language family falls. She learns to use vocabulary, idioms, manner of speaking, posture, and gesture common to her family, neighborhood, school, and peer group. She edits or expands her speech according to the age, sex, and status of those with whom she is dealing. She learns when to speak and when not to, how to be tactful, and how to be sarcastic. And because she is a problem-solver, she is flexible, adapting what she says to various situations and matching her knowledge to her experience in order to comprehend.

The child most often operates on a practical plane. As her knowledge of the world grows, she learns how to make the most economical use of the cues received from her experiences. A cartoon person from the 1980 season of Sesame Street sang a song based on this concept.

> My name is Fred.
> They call me Fred.
> When I go out
> I put a hat upon my _____.

> My name is Fred.
> They call me Fred.
> When I sit down to eat
> I butter up a slice of _____.

> My name is Fred.
> They call me Fred.
> Every night when I get tired
> I go to _____.

Children have little difficulty supplying the missing words, because they have put hats on their heads, buttered bread, and gone to bed. These life experiences allow them to guess at the meaning and respond quickly (Smith, 1971). Moreover, the first two lines are repeated and the missing words must rhyme with Fred. Therefore, cues in the linguistic structure, accompanied by a simple beat, help children predict the words necessary to complete the verses.

While language is predictable, it is also generative. It is astounding that from various combinations of 26 letters and 40-odd phonemes, we get the words in an unabridged English dictionary. Language not only reinforces our experiences, but it also reorders our perceptions as well as our idioms and vocabulary as our experiences expand our knowledge of the world. The generative or creative power of language therefore increases its predictive domain. We continue to learn during our entire lives through speaking and listening and, in a print laden society, through reading and writing. We grow and change, and our language grows and changes with us. Living is itself a process. Thus, language as a means for survival, growth, and pleasure is likewise a process.

Talking, Reading, and Writing

Children learn to talk in a setting which is usually relaxed. Parents, relatives, babysitters, and nursery school teachers talk with children about topics of interest during ongoing activities, using the immediate context to aid communication. The children interact with peers and adults, and the adults present do not discourage the children from taking their time, starting over, rewording, hesitating, or ending in mid-sentence. The children's need to communicate is immediate, necessary, and inevitable. However, while all capable children learn to use oral language, not all learn to handle written language.

Traditional attitudes toward literacy education foster this discrepancy. Succumbing to the notion that literacy requires formal instruction, teachers often discourage parents from exposing preschoolers to reading on the grounds that they will confuse the children, make school more difficult for them later on, damage their vision, or cause them to be bored with school activities (Emery, 1975). Postponing experience with reading for children who are interested creates self-doubt about how this mystical ability is acquired. When we introduce experiences that do not promote relevant encounters with print, and particularly in an atmosphere which includes negative remarks and punishment for taking time, rephrasing, or mispronouncing, we destroy the children's desire to explore and their freedom to guess, strategies that have stood them well in handling the world since birth. Thus, children learn that previous experiences are no help in school and reading becomes an empty, painful experience.

Usually writing assignments are peripheral exercises varying from ultimate control in copying to absolute freedom in such essays as "What I Did During My Summer Vacation." The children's spelling and grammar are often more heavily evaluated than their ideas and rarely do they have the opportunity to read aloud and share what they have written. Moreover, writing the same sentence again and again may still be punishment for deviations from expected classroom behavior. Faced with empty writing exercises in an environment where they experience inadequacy, children decide that the acquisition of writing is not meaningful in their lives and lose interest in trying to learn to write.

Often educational programs fail to view oral and written language as complementary modes of expression within an individual's overall communicative model. Even more basically, those who design and determine curriculum fail to perceive it as a dynamic process, responsive to the changing culture and society and the developing individual. The goal of education should be to help the child *do* rather than to teach some *thing* to the child. We listen and talk in order to learn how to listen and talk, and we engage in reading and writing in order to learn how to read and write. This approach can only be handled by a philosophy of reading and writing which is flexible, adaptive, and comprehension centered. The traditional disciplines then become part of the lifelong learning of the individual and, rather then isolated subject matter, reading and writing become the problem solving, information processing events they are.

The Return to Process

A growing number of educators are adjusting the focus of their attention from learner performance to learner competence, which is a shift from product to process. The rationale of this shift lies in the assumption that children are able to observe, categorize, associate, hypothesize, revise, integrate information, and solve problems. These learning strategies enable them not only to think and to talk, but also to become literate. Oral and written language develop then as constructive processes, reflective of the particular culture that gives rise to them. These processes respond to meaningful experiences, and they in turn aid the cultivation of the learning strategies. With its roots in psycholinguistics, this perspective has gained acceptance at national levels.

Demonstrating such an orientation, the 1979 and 1980 conventions of the International Reading Association and the National Council of Teachers of English cosponsored workshops relating research on child language development to language arts curriculum in the schools. By exploring what learners know, these workshops proposed that educators nurture positive encounters with print much the same as parents facilitate oral language growth. Among the traditional language arts, the field of reading has frequently been criticized by its own members as insufficiently theoretical and by outsiders as failing to produce an effective method of teaching reading. "An argument for research" (*Reading Research Quarterly,* 9, 2, 1973-1974, editorial) states that "...one of the major problems has been that too little is known about reading as a process or how children learn to read." The study of a child in the early stages of oral language development experiencing her first encounters with written language could therefore provide insight into the actual nature of reading and writing, and indicate ways in which traditional instructional basics may be improved.

The Rationale for a Case Study

The case study is one method commonly used in learning about individuals. According to Rothney (1968), the case study is the procedure under which all other methods may be subsumed, since testing, interviewing, describing, and analyzing are employed in the collection of data for a case study. Barr (1930) states that because the case study is essentially a combination of the causal, historical, and experimental methods of research, it has more continuity with human life. Diesing (1971) emphasizes that since the researcher is at home with a subject that reacts and initiates while participating in a vivid and fulfilling communicative event, the case study "...gets at something real that other methods miss" (p. 286).

Good (1941) maintains that the case study is particularly adapted to the analysis of complex phenomena under real life and/or controlled conditions. As a holistic approach which preserves the subject's dignity, the case study investigates the internal dynamics of a living system (Diesing, 1971). The researcher examines the subject, who is an active participant in self-development, from an integrative, constructive viewpoint. The essence of the method is not only the collection of objective data, which is assumed, but the inference of relationships among the data and of the data to external information (Barr, 1930). Rothney (1968) supports this characteristic of the approach by requiring continuous conceptualization on the part of the researcher while organizing the data. Since we expect an inquiry to be carried out so that a certain audience will benefit, case studies are more in harmony with the reader's experience and for this reason a natural basis for generalization (Stake, 1978).

Research on child language has developed theory using the case study as its primary method and focusing on stages of development common to various cases. In contrast, research on reading has usually emphasized application. More often the setting for reading research has been the classroom where language is taught formally to large groups, and where language structure rather than natural communicative intent is the focus. Here, primary attention is paid to the manipulation of the structure and the presentation of teaching materials. However, most case studies have depended on natural settings where oral language is learned because of communicative needs. Their primary focus is on the strategies of the learner (Ervin-Tripp, 1974). Whenever case studies in reading have appeared, they have been limited recollections of difficulties or teacher reports (Miel, 1958). Yet it is possible to discern longer descriptive studies in reports of early readers (Cohan, 1961; Fowler, 1962; Söderbergh, 1971) and several recent dissertations (Andrews, 1976; Y. Goodman, 1967; McKenzie, 1974).

Case studies of single children learning oral language include well-known diary accounts (Darwin, 1877; Leopold, 1939-1949; Prior, 1894; Shinn, 1893; Sully, 1895; Taine, 1877), and descriptive accounts of single children learning to read are also notable (Cohan, 1961; Fowler, 1962; Francis, 1975; Söderbergh, 1971; Terman, 1918). Bissex (1980) documents the intertwined relations of learning to read and learning to write through a five year case study, begun when the child was 5½ years old. While a case study of one child may be limited in generalizability to larger populations, with a sufficient number of such long term case studies, generalizations have the opportunity to be validated (Cook-Gumperz and Corsaro, 1977). In fact, the *Annual Summary of Investigations Relating to Reading, July 1, 1979 to June 30, 1980,* p. viii, notes such an increase in the number of intensive studies of individual subjects that the study of one child is no longer suspect or even unusual.

Parent Case Studies

In the study of child language, the relation of the investigator to the child is extremely important (Francis, 1975). Since there is no consensus as to the nature of the phenomena of language acquisition, the reading process, or the writing process, the observer imposes interpretation on whatever she observes as an essential activity. While interacting with the child, the observer must make the distinction between her observations and any subjectivity stemming from the relationship with the child or from emotion present in the collecting situation. Bissex (1980) introduces the five year case study she conducted on her son by stating that such methodology is "...an attempt to understand another person through enlightened subjectivity" (p. vi). While a parent is inherently subjective, a formally trained parent brings to the task the enlightenment that comes from years of training in a particular field. A detailed case study of a child learning language would be virtually impossible for a nonparent researcher. No other person will ever know the child, the context of the child's life, and the particular research situation so completely as the parent (Fowler, 1962). No one but a parent would have the opportunity.

Researchers in oral language acquisition, who were parents, typically capitalized on such opportunities by studying their own children (Darwin, 1877; Leopold, 1939-1949). The First International Symposium on First Language Acquisition in Florence in 1972 emphasized the important role parent studies have played and continue to play in studying the phenomenon of language. As a researcher in reading and writing, who is a parent, I consider the case study a worthwhile methodology in my own area of interest. Deciding that an infant encountering print was as basic as an investigation of literacy could go, I observed the actions, audio- and videotaped the reading and writing interactions, and collected the writing and drawing samples of our daughter from birth to three years of age. I have made every effort to maintain objectivity while capitalizing on my close relations with Giti.

Procedure

A diary was kept of the actual experiences involving both elicited and spontaneous utterances and observations and inferences concerning Giti's approaches to oral and written language. A sample tape recording of our reading interactions was compiled each month on one cassette as well as a videotape of an experience with written language. All of Giti's writing samples were dated, described, and preserved, and any distinction she made between writing and drawing was recorded. Procedures for the analysis of these data were both longitudinal, drawing parallels between oral language acquisition and learning to read and write, and qualitative, depending on the functions for which Giti used linguistic structures with print (see Appendix 1 for Procedure Summary).

Since caregiver language to a child is qualitatively different (Bruner, 1978; Brown, 1973; Bullowa, 1964; Drach, 1969; Fraser, 1975; Snow, 1973), my speech to Giti was also tape recorded and transcribed. Our interactions were not only recorded and transcribed by me, but also observed and documented by a third person, Giti's father. Such documentation is particularly important because mothers typically interact with infants using a conversational model, and the often unconscious changes in their speech reflect the growing ability of the child to function as a conversational partner (Bruner, 1978; Snow, 1973). The hours spent together each day were recorded and averaged on a daily, weekly, and monthly basis.

Related Research

Language Acquisition: Basic Positions

Interest in child language may be documented at least as early as 610 B.C. when, according to legend, James VI of Scotland placed two infants on an uninhabited island in the care of a deaf-mute nursemaid in order to discover humankind's first language, that is, the language which Adam and Eve spoke (Deese, 1970, p. 53). But systematic research on child language begins in the nineteenth century with diaries kept by parents (Darwin, 1877; Prior, 1894; Shinn, 1893; Sully, 1895; Taine, 1877). In the twentieth century, descriptive observations of language in the context of total child development shift to purely linguistic themes, comparing child language to an adult model (Brandenburg, 1915; Cooley, 1908; Leopold, 1939-49; Nice, 1915; Stern, 1924), and by the 1960s definite perspectives emerge as to why children learn to speak and why they follow much the same patterns of language development.

Behavioral psychologists are mainly interested in the prediction and control of functional units of behavior. Skinner (1957) accepts the capacities of association formation and stimulus response generalization as native properties of the human organism, but argues that language is merely behavior which human beings reinforce, and language in turn reinforces learning through its effects on human beings. The child is therefore born *tabula rasa*, and acquires language as a sophisticated response system through processes of conditioning. Children apply universal principles of learning to the raw data of their experiences, and the environment rewards them for linguistic conformity while ignoring or punishing them for linguistic deviations. Language is thus handled in much the same way as all learned behavior, and it is the essential similarity among environments that accounts for observed sameness in general laws of learning. Critics of this viewpoint acknowledge that reinforcement, inquisitiveness, hypothesis testing, and generalization have their places in language acquisition, but as Noam Chomsky (1965) claims, no single strategy nor all strategies together can account for what actually happens in language learning. Children learn abstract structures for which no overt word-order patterns exist in the data to which they are exposed.

Nativists claim many more endowments for the child. Chomsky (1965) assumes that the child's ability to produce and understand novel sentences relies on an innate capacity, and the child acquires language by discovering its underlying system of grammatical rules. McNeill (1970) goes farther by stating that before language acquisition even begins, the child possesses some knowledge of grammatical categories and their relations as well as the notion that sentences are represented by deep and surface structures through an innate language acquisition device or LAD. Relying heavily on data from evolutionary theory and biological sciences, Lenneberg (1967) emphasizes that language is a species-specific behavior intimately related to the maturation of the uniquely human physiology, and that between the ages of two and twelve years there is a critical, biologically determined period for language acquisition. Other supportive evidence for the concept of a critical period for learning language comes from studies of language universals, which assume that human languages share features because all humans share specific learning capacities (Slobin, 1968b). For example, a sentence may be turned into a question or a command, or it may be negated. These forms in different languages may be different, but the functional patterns of the transformations are similar throughout the world. While none of the arguments conclusively proves the case of elaborate language-processing abilities, nativists do inquire into the ability of the child to go beyond the examples heard in the environment.

These behaviorist and nativist views of language acquisition are as opposed as any popular debate of nurture versus nature. Behaviorists emphasize principles of learning and the environment to the neglect of the learner and her language, while nativists stress the internal mechanisms of the learner relatively independent of experiential influences. Both perspectives, respectively preoccupied with behavior and grammar, have traditionally neglected the original historical orientation of language in the total situational context as used by the child.

Sociolinguists state that in addition to the child's acquisition of the structural rules of her language, she must also learn social editing, that is, when she should or should not speak and which linguistic code she should use (Hymes, 1967a; Williams & Naremore, 1969). As part of this communicative competence, sociolinguists examine the child's learning environment in order to locate possible sources of influence on her language development. This environmentalist position is differentiated from both the behaviorist and nativist positions in that it recognizes individual and group differences in language learning which act as external forces on the internal mechanisms of the speaker-learner.

From a cognitivist perspective, children are born possessing sets of procedures and inference rules which combine with memory to enable them to handle linguistic data. The ensuing mental development then determines the acquisition of language. Slobin (1966) maintains that strictly linguistic acquisition may be completed by about three years of age and continued development in language might simply reflect the lifting of performance restrictions and general cognitive growth. His evidence from the acquisition of different languages indicates that semantic ability develops fairly consistently across languages with similar cognitive limitations on the expression of concepts. Apparently children everywhere search out ways to express more and more complicated meanings, relying on innate abilities to guide what they look for and their strategies. The Swiss psychologist, Piaget, maintained lifelong interest in universal patterns of cognitive growth. Trained as a biologist and experienced as a researcher in human intelligence, he postulates that the child is an active organism innately structured to develop according to a fixed pattern. To test the hypothesis that cognitive development directs language development, he had children pour a fixed quantity of liquid into containers of various shapes, and then asked each time if the resulting container held more or less than the amount with which they started. Children who did not understand the principle of conservation, that is, the quantity does not change with the shape of the container, could not use comparatives in speech. It was also very difficult to teach the nonconservers the terms used by the conservers. Parallels between Piaget's descriptions of the establishment of basic categories of thought during the sensorimotor period and the basic semantic relations expressed in early sentences have also been drawn (Bloom, 1973; Brown, 1973). However, Sinclair-deZwart (1973), who has worked with Piaget, notes that a direct transposition of his theory of cognitive development to psycholinguistics is no easy task.

In summary, there is a strong biological component in language acquisition. The environment provides the opportunities for its realization, and the pace of acquisition itself is controlled by the developing complexity of the children who are doing the acquiring. Therefore, the process of language acquisition must be studied in conjunction with the acquisition of other kinds of knowledge and abilities, namely those that involve biological, intellectual, and social development, for it is the interaction of all these factors which determines linguistic growth.

Semantic Analyses of Language

The meaning of a word can be defined by semantic characteristics which differentiate that word from others. Clark (1973) applies the Semantic Features Hypothesis to the acquisition of first words by stating that initially the child attaches words to only one or two features of a word's referents and gradually adds features until the adult meaning is obtained. Thus, percepts are transferred directly to semantics, which accounts for identification of referents, but which does not account for concept development independent of lexical meaning. Gibson and Levin (1975) criticize her application by stating that, like distinctive features in phonology, semantic features are contrastive. They conclude that the word *dog* is simply another characteristic of a familiar object, and when the child applies the word *dog* to *cow* and receives feedback, there is a basis for abstracting the semantic features which distinguish the animals. At an early stage of language development, the features become lists that help the learner define categories found in her environment.

To combine syntactic and semantic features of sentences, Fillmore (1968) postulates a theory of case grammar. This approach is based on universal, presumably innate concepts derived from human judgments concerning such matters as who did something, to whom it happened, and what was changed. The first set of cases he proposed deals with perceptual invariants every listener or reader experiences: Agentive (A); Instrumental (I); Dative (D); Factitive (F): Locative (L); and Objective (O). Brown (1973) has found Fillmore's case grammar useful for understanding the first stages of language development, particularly verbs, and further defines and adds to the six basic cases. Case relations have been criticized for blurring the distinction between meaning and syntax so that some cases, such as (O) Objective, become catchalls for items that do not quite fit into any of the other cases.

The Semantic Revolution refers to the trend whereby linguistics began to supplement grammatical descriptions of the emerging language of children with broader descriptions of the context of such utterances. Bloom (1970) recorded two occasions of a child saying, "mommy sock." With the then prevailing child grammar rules, both utterances would have been classified pivot word + open class word. However, in one context, the child was picking up and identifying her mother's stocking (possession), while in the other context the mother was attempting to put the child's sock on her daughter (action). Bloom decided that analyzing utterances merely in terms of grammatical rules fails to accurately describe the structure of these utterances and her final analysis includes an interpretation of the meaning of the utterance from her observations of the immediate context in which it occurred. Schlesinger (1971) combines generative grammar and semantics to emphasize that when writing grammars for children, general knowledge about the world should be distinguished from linguistically relevant knowledge. He develops the I-marker or intention marker to represent in the analysis those cognitive relations which make a difference linguistically. In fact, he declares that not only is semantic intent the precursor of a child's utterances, but that such intent is the basis of the units in which children generate their grammar, i.e. semantic grammar.

Schema theory assumes that spoken or written text does not in itself carry meaning but provides directions on how to reconstruct the intended meaning (Hacker, 1980). As a description of a particular class of concepts, it is composed of a hierarchy of schemata embedded within schemata. At the top of the hierarchy the representation is abstract. Moving down the hierarchy, the schemata apply to unique perceptual events. Because every schema specifies interrelationships, once an element is named it can be understood in its proper context through bottom-up or top-down processing, and the process of interpretation is guided by the principle that all data must be accounted for. Each input event must be mapped against some schema and all aspects of the schema must be compatible with the input information. Because hierarchial structuring may underlie cognitive processes, and schema theory provides a way of integrating understanding of spoken or written text with our understanding of the world (Adams & Collins, 1977), schema theory offers applications to the study of child language.

Some attention has been directed at the effect the entire communication act has on the form and context of children's utterances. Speech act theory provides a way of talking about utterances

> In terms of the context in which they are made, the intentions, attitudes, and expectations of the participants, the relationships existing between the participants, and generally the unspoken rules and conventions that are understood to be in play when an utterance is made and received. (Pratt, 1977, p. 86)

Bruner (1975c) adopts a speech act approach in order to consider language in relation to general behavior and to allow emphasis on the use of language rather than its form. Drawing examples from early mother-infant interaction, he analyzes intention into measurable features and distinguishes mastery play (infant-object play facilitated by an adult but not dependent on adult reciprocity) from reciprocal play. His crucial point is that eye games or "gaze coupling," draw the child's attention to the communication itself and to the structure of the acts in which the communication is taking place. Cook-Gumperz (1975) agrees that social understandings which give the child grounds for formulating semantic intentions trigger the acquisition of syntax. A principle of reciprocity, in which the child understands that the world is shared, leads to the process of building up a set of grammatical rules from context bound messages in which setting, paralinguistic features, and verbal message all contribute to the meaning. As a practical reasoner, the child fills in previous experience to make sense of the verbal messages received. The principle of reciprocity causes the child to give and to expect understanding from another person. As the notion of foregrounding (i.e. features of communicative acts that can usually be taught or described) develops, the child learns that language can provide the grounds for its own understanding as well. If language acquisition can be seen as a process of realizing the normative character of a shared world rather than simply a linguistic and/or cognitive process, Cook-Gumperz proposes that linguistic work can be integrated into a single social framework. Halliday (1975b) provides a detailed model of language functions and the relations between language knowledge and social interaction. He investigates how children construct social reality through use of language while maintaining meaning. Children know what language is because they know what language does and as "a rich and adaptable instrument," there is hardly any limit to what children can do with it. As a result, a child's model of language is complex and might better be thought of as models to emphasize the many-sidedness of developing linguistic experience. Even as Halliday classifies the earliest utterances as instrumental, regulatory, and interactional, he admits that they mean what they mean because that is how the adult involved understands the utterances. A constant problem in a functionalist paradigm is how to distinguish between children's intentions and adult interpretations of their intentions.

Historically, language studies begin with descriptions of contextual usage, proceed to analyses of phonological, morphological or syntactic components of language, and achieve isolated self-containment with Chomsky's perception of the formal nature of language. As a reaction to studies of language taken out of context, scholars begin to turn toward considerations of language use. This perspective might be considered going full circle to the recording of context, except that such theorists occasionally become so concerned with the use of the utterance that they too are guilty of relegating the producer of the utterance and individual learning strategies to a minimal role. As yet, theorists have failed to produce a successful model of what is happening linguistically, in terms of a comprehensive description of the situation, which also grants an equal share to the contribution made by the learner. Moreover, in terms of models and analyses in the acquisition of language by children, no approach clearly distinguishes child language from adult language.

Early Readers

Despite the emphasis on literacy and the availability of commercial programs, we seem to know least about the beginning phase of reading and beginning reading as it relates to speaking. Yet both learning to speak and learning to read base their activities on the communication of meaning. If we agree that speaking progresses faster than reading because of its immediate relevance in the life of a child, then the child cannot read better than she can organize her ideas and express them in speech. Because interpreting and reacting to printed language can be a short step from interpreting and reacting to spoken language, oral language growth should be a primary concern when considering beginning reading (Artley, 1953). Traditionally, studies specifically concerned with the relation between oral language and reading compare children learning to talk in a natural setting to children learning to read in a formal setting (Carroll, 1966; Samuels, 1978), concentrate on children in first grade subject to interference from instructional programs (Bull, 1974; Hildreth, 1963), or review theoretical aspects of the processes apart from real children (Athey, 1971a). In all cases, correlations between learning to talk and learning to read have not been clearly drawn.

The investigation of learning to read should focus on what is happening within the child. "If the child must essentially 'do it herself,' what will make her do it, keep her at it, and tell her when she has perceived a useful relation?" (Gibson & Levin, 1975, p. 265). Bruner (1966) defines this drive as "the will to learn." We are attracted to something that is unclear, unfinished, or uncertain, and set out to understand it and put it in order (Day, Berlyne, & Hunt, 1971). The urge to control causes children to practice language on their own (Weir, 1962). As a result of much exposure to meaningful language as part of a total environment, positive reinforcement, and opportunity for experimenting through hypothesis testing and self-evaluation, children learn oral language (Hall &

Ramig, 1978). And children apply concepts and strategies attained through oral language development to print.

When parents of natural readers were asked to identify characteristics which differentiated their early reader from siblings in physical development, they could not. Early readers did not appear to be superior to their siblings in walking, talking, or toilet training (Clark, 1976). Durkin (1966) finds that the parents she interviewed described the personal characteristics of both early readers and nonearly readers as similar. These children had good memories and were able to focus their concentration on a task for some time. In addition, they appeared to be curious, conscientious, serious, persistent, and self-reliant. Clark (19760) notes that early readers enjoyed the company of adults as well as other children, and when others were not available they seemed content to play alone. Neither is high IQ a necessary prerequisite for early reading. Durkin (1966, p. 134) found the median IQs of the two large groups she studied to be high, but the range was quite large (91-161 in California and 82-170 in New York), and Clark (1976) cites examples where IQ cannot totally explain early reading acquisition.

However, in contrasting parental perceptions of early readers' handling of written language with siblings who do not read, Clark (1976, p. 93) finds that the early reader does not make out the sounds of the letters and work out words, "pronouncing like a child," but rather "it just click(s)," so that there seems to be a qualitative difference in the processing strategies of preschool readers. Briggs and Elkind (1973) assess the logical abilities of preschool readers with a control group of matched nonearly readers to argue that, within the Piagetian framework, if logical abilities are a necessary condition for learning to read, then early readers should be superior to nonreaders in concrete operations. They find that "...early readers, regardless of intellectual levels, tended to be significantly higher than their matched controls on measures of perceptual regulations and concrete operations" (Elkind, 1974a, p. 194). King and Friesen (1972) compare kindergarten readers with a group of randomly selected nonreaders in the same age range across 13 variables and find that the selected skills are more differentiated for early readers and that the reading-related skills are more distinct for the preschool readers. These early readers are able to direct their own learning by asking appropriate questions about print (Clark, 1976; Durkin, 1966; Torrey, 1973), and this self-instruction apparently takes place even when the child's environment does not necessarily facilitate learning (Torrey, 1973).

Early readers come from various social classes and have parents with varying degrees of education. The most common characteristic of their early home environment is a warm and accepting atmosphere where the child is valued as an individual. Plessas and Oakes (1964), Durkin (1966), and Clark (1976) found that one or both of the parents of early readers were avid readers themselves. These family members accepted and responded to what the child was trying to do. Durkin (1966) and Clark (1976) emphasize that parents and older siblings answered questions about the words the children saw in books, newspapers, and signs in an encouraging yet casual interaction.

Durkin's studies (1966) of early readers demonstrate easy access to a wide variety of reading materials, especially storybooks. Clark (1976) adds that availability also includes extensive use of the local library. The range of printed materials is not confined to books. Durkin (1966), Clark (1976), and Wiseman (1980) cite the importance of noticing everyday print such as billboards, captions, products at the supermarket, and labels. These various types of print encourage learning to read as a component of trying to comprehend the environment (Teale, 1978).

Reading to children is repeatedly mentioned as a factor in the learning environment of early readers (Baghban, 1979; Butler & Clay, 1979; Clark, 1976; Durkin, 1966; Kohl, 1973; Mason, 1980; Mass, 1981; McKenzie, 1977; Moffett & Wagner, 1976; Plessas & Oakes, 1964). Children learning to read at home have most commonly learned through the lap method (Moffett & Wagner, 1976, p. 186, 202). Children sit on the reader's lap or beside the reader and listen to a story while following the book with their eyes. As children follow the story, they match it to the print grossly at first and then refine it (Mason, 1980; Moffett & Wagner, 1976). In addition to identification and refinement of print, the developing sense of story helps children make an entity of experience and generalizations about the operation of the world. Beginning at approximately 2½ years of age, children can use this story schema to aid comprehension of both conversation and print (Applebee, 1978; Brown, 1977).

The environment of the early reader also facilitates contact with paper and pencil (Hildreth, 1963; Kohl, 1973; Teale, 1978). Durkin's early (1966) readers move in sequence from scribbling and drawing to copying letters to questions about spelling. The children in her studies are termed "paper and pencil children" because of their own early interest in playing with drawing and writing. Clay's observations (1977) of infant classrooms lead her to the conclusion that when child discovery is valued and creative writing encouraged, writing plays a significant role in early reading. Plessas and Oakes (1964) and Clark (1976) also emphasize early readers' preoccupation with copying and printing.

Despite all this positive experience with print, some children still are not early readers, and the same family may produce both early readers and nonreaders (Clark, 1976). None of the outlined characteristics is limited to early readers, but these traits were commonly found among early readers. Rather then determiners, these characteristics appear to be contributors to a total picture.

Early Writers

According to Cattell's (1960) scale of infant intelligence, the average child will scribble spontaneously when given paper and pencil at 18 months, or earlier if given a demonstration of how to write. Legrun (1932) and Hildreth (1936) note stages of development in writing which begin with unorganized scribbles and then proceed to scribbles with vertical and horizontal tendencies, consistent linearity, unbroken structures, and units with real or approximations to real letters. Given the proper tools, children will scribble, draw, and print spontaneously, differentiate pictorial information from graphic information, and learn the distinctive features used in writing on their own (Gibson & Levin, 1975). Clay (1975) demonstrates that a 2-year-old will scribble for the enjoyment of movement or for the visually satisfying marks that appear. But somewhere between the ages of three and five years, most children become aware that people make marks on paper purposefully. Initially, children may produce scribble writing, linear mock writing, or mock letters. Then, as children direct their attention to print, they may trace over script, copy print, and remember alphabet symbols. Gradually, children use the relationships between the sounds and letters to spell what they understand (Chomsky, 1976; Gentry, 1978, 1981; Read, 1971; Zutell, 1978). Read (1971) demonstrates that although children are actually more proficient than adults in sounding out words, their spellings often appear strange because they have not learned (as literate adults have) to ignore some very real similarities in sounds. He uses his findings to emphasize that young children naturally have a highly sophisticated intuitive understanding of phonology which they use in their invented spellings.

Read (1975b) identifies common characteristics of children who invent spellings. He notes that they learned the conventional names of the alphabet letters at a relatively early age, even as young as 2.6 years. Most of the children played with letter blocks or a movable alphabet tray, and began to spell single words usually between 3.0 and 4.6 years. They enacted the use of paper and pencil, and their parents were generally responsive and interested.

Five spelling stages are found in the writing development of natural readers (Beers & Beers, 1980; Beers & Henderson, 1977; Gentry, 1978). The initial babbling stage for the early writer has been dubbed the deviant stage. It is the child's first attempt to write with an alphabet and demonstrates a random ordering of the letters the child is able to produce from recall. Responses may range from an approximation of real letters to true letters interspersed with numerals written in random order from left to right, e.g. b+BpA=monster. Children demonstrate no knowledge of letter-sound correspondence and cannot later read their samples (Gentry, 1978, 1981).

As children begin forming concepts of the alphabetic principle, they link letters to sounds. In this prephonetic stage, children omit vowels and use one, two, or three consonants that demonstrate letter-sound correspondence, e.g. MSR = monster; TP = type (Gentry, 1981).

The phonetic stage which follows stabilizes children's linking of letter to sound. The system is concrete, frequently matching sounds to letter names, e.g. MONSTR = monster, CHROBL = trouble, TIP = type, ATE = eighty (Beers & Henderson, 1977; Gentry, 1978, 1981).

As phonetic writers become better acquainted with standard orthography, their representations become more abstract. They advance to a transitional stage between phonetic and correct spelling. Though often misspelled, children's words do look like English, with vowels in every syllable. They display knowledge of common vowel patterns, e.g. TIPE = type, TODE = toad (Gentry, 1978, 1981). Inflectional endings are spelled uniformly for the first time.

In the correct stage, children recognize and recall the correct lexical representation. The entire word is spelled correctly. Gentry (1981) advises no formal teaching of spelling until the attainment of this developmental stage, and Chomsky (1970) advises the teaching of spelling by word families, comparisons, and contrasts so that learners can build on the discovered hypotheses about how print operates.

Based on their encounters with print, children develop expectancies not only for the form but also for the function of their written products. They write lists, notes, letters, stories, and books, and they are able to demonstrate the differing formats of their expressions. Harste and Carey (1979) support Megan's understanding of the overall organization of her written language by contrasting her demonstrated perception of the elements of a story (protagonist, attempt, consequence) with her production of a letter (salutation, body, signature). In environments that immerse these children in print and allow them to discover, formulate, test, and develop hypotheses about orthography, the children determine a role for their written products. To keep them producing, adults need therefore to read children's products for the message they carry rather than for their conformity to graphic conventions (Clay, 1975).

Many theorists see writing as an exploratory activity to accompany reading (Burke, 1972; Clay, 1977; Goodman, 1970; Moffett & Wagner, 1976; Paul, 1976). Hildreth (1963) and Carroll (1966) agree that reading and writing activities be used to support each other in instructional settings. Durkin (1966, 1974-1975) indicates that the starting point for her subjects was an interest in copying letters of the alphabet. Once children are writing, they will ask questions about the spellings of words and will read. Chomsky (1971, 1972b) declares that the natural order of learning is for children to write before reading. She states that, at first, children will not be able to read what they have produced, but whenever they reach the point of being able to read their own productions, they will be easier to read because the written word grows out of the children's consciousness and belongs to them. True preparation for reading is in making their own productions before they are expected to read other people's productions. Likewise, Ashton-Warner (1963) supports the creation of individual productions before encountering other people's productions by requiring, as do British infant schools, that each pupil make a book before receiving a manufactured text.

Drawing as a Language Art

The construction of meaning from the perception of patterned stimuli is a universal in human life and a skill necessary for survival (Eisner, 1978). Cognitive processes develop while contexts vary. We learn to read print and pictures in order to construct meaning, and we compose print and pictures in order to communicate meaning. Art stimulates a child's natural curiosity and may even literally expand the capacity of the brain, as in the case of Chris (Williams, 1977).

> In the early grades of a public elementary school, her mother says, "Chris got passed along although she wasn't reading and didn't know her math concepts." Enrolled at Mead in the fourth grade, she did almost nothing but artwork for the first year; that was just as well, because she developed a passion for math, and her math grades improved rapidly. Her other grades began improving also. At the end of sixth grade, she was testing at the seventh and eighth grade levels in all subjects. Now a high school senior, she gets all A's and B's and is headed toward a career in art. (p. 16)

Chris was able to take advantage of the flexibility in art to demonstrate improvement in traditional academic subjects. Drawing was verbal implications. Because drawing is expressive, its composing processes complement writing and speaking, and because the interpretation of pictures is receptive, drawing complements reading and listening. Researchers who have chronicled stages in the development of drawing in young children emphasize the connection between the ability to create basic gestalts in art and the ability to read quickly and well (Goodnow, 1977; Kellogg, 1977).

In summary, children younger than six (and they do not need to be especially bright or from upperclass families) are teaching themselves to read and write by asking the right questions and experimenting with print and drawing in contexts that are pleasant and interesting. A significant, positive relationship exists between children's positive responses to opportunities to examine and produce written language in relaxed settings prior to first grade and success in beginning reading in school (Almy, 1950), and children who read early tend to maintain their lead over classmates who do not begin to read until first grade (Durkin, 1966, 1972).

Oral Language and Reading

Giti was born on August 5, 1976, the first child of Hafiz and Marcia Baghban. We lived in a one bedroom apartment (see Appendix II) in married student housing on the campus of Indiana University, where her father, whom she calls /baba/, was Visiting Assistant Professor of Folklore and I was a graduate student in reading education. I was primarily responsible for her care during the first three years of life, with the exception of Summer 1979. Giti's father, who worked nearly 60 hours a week during the early part of her life, assumed much of the responsibility for care in Summer 1979. Her maternal grandparents, Mary and Frederick Moses, visited when Giti was born (one week), when she was 3 months old (one week), 6 months (three weeks), 14 months (one week), 18 months (one month), 26 months (one month), and 31 months (one month). During the last three visits (one month each) her grandparents assumed total responsibility for her care from 10 a.m. to 5 p.m. daily. Giti's friends were youngsters in university housing ranging in age from 3 months to 5 years. She played with these preschoolers as often as possible.

Both parents and grandparents supported Giti's learning. We read to her whenever she wanted; took her to the library, restaurants, and stores; talked to her; asked her questions; answered her questions; pointed out and named objects; and praised her. While Giti might occasionally hear Dari, or Afghan Persian, used by her father with friends or see letters arriving in Persian, the oral language addressed to her and the writing conducted in front of her was in English.

A conscious decision was made to introduce Giti to reading by reading to her, but no direct teaching of a particular method of reading instruction or of the alphabet as the alphabet was undertaken. In addition, no handmade books, with the exception of logos that she recognized at 25 months, were used in order to assure ease in replication and generalization of this project (see the Bibliography of Giti's Books). The reading and writing samples included in this study are the best representatives taken from the extensive materials collected from Giti.

When reading to Giti, we usually held her on our laps. If I was sitting alone and Giti wanted me to read, she would select a book, stand in front of me and back up with book in hand. Giti did this with her father as well and with visitors after she got to know them. As she grew into reading in the morning, she would climb into bed next to us, share the pillow, and hand over a book to be read. Grandparents usually sat next to her when reading and as Giti became larger, she occasionally wanted to sit next to us, but close enough for her to lean on us and for us to have an arm around her. I consciously would direct Giti into sitting on my lap even as she grew older because we both enjoyed the physical contact and it seemed to enhance the person-to-person communication inherent in early reading (see Appendix 3 for transcription of sample interactions).

Observations

As any infant, Giti was born into the world with the instinct to survive. She found that crying got her a dry diaper, something to ease her stomach, and company at three in the morning. She learned to differentiate her cries and to wait for responses. Fulfillment of basic needs, reinforced daily by eye contact with the caregivers, helped her realize that she was not along in the world, that some kind of bridging goes on from one human being to another (Bruner, 1978). Gradually, she learned that speech was different from noise and that these sounds referred to objects, people, and events. By the age of three months, with the added perspective of sitting upright, she could also pause, gesture, and look around expecting a response. From this time on, she used her utterances not only to satisfy basic needs, but to actively discover the someone who, through her experience, had been alleviating her discomfort. She grunted, gurgled and cooed, using smiling and pointing, like me, to supplement conversations. At first, the interpretation and maintenance of such dialogue required a great deal of effort on my part, but slowly Giti assumed more of the responsibility for initiating and maintaining conversations. She used language to get a handle on her world. She learned to take turns, and true dialogue became the major vehicle for her language development.

Giti's early reading experience was also interactive. She sat on my lap and we both assumed roles and took turns. However, rather than the luxury of choosing a topic from the larger environment, in this instance, the book determined the topic and the direction of the interaction. Giti received *Pat the Bunny* at nine months. *Pat the Bunny* is predictable and appeals to the child's orientation to action and participation. After the text was read and demonstrated to her just one time, she was able to assume the role of "you" whenever it might be read. Cloth books and a *Mother Goose* with cardboard pages were then added to her library. These books allowed questions on details in the pictures ("Do you see the _____?"), commands ("Look at the _____."), and comments ("Isn't the cat funny!"). Any response which Giti made in action or speech was met with, "Yes," "That's right," or "Good." By 12 months, her book handling behavior was clearly established. She could flip books rightside up, turn pages from left to right, and favor particular pictures by banging on them with her hands, keeping the book open to certain pages, or locating favorite pages. In addition to traditional caretaker-child rhymes such as "Peek-a-Boo" and "This Little Piggy," the introduction of *Mother Goose* permitted participation in "Pat-a Cake" and song equivalents in "Ring Around the Rosie," "Mary Had a Little Lamb," "London Bridge," and "Yankee Doodle." These rhymes could be sung while cleaning, riding in the car, or taking a walk, and Giti frequently instigated the chorus by babbling in song herself. Each time she encountered the text, she demonstrated that she knew which pages could be sung. When these rhymes came, she sang, clapped, and usually refused to turn the page until she tired of the more familiar rhyme. Later, introduction of the texts to *Old MacDonald Had a Farm* and *The Mulberry Bush* provided the same interaction between song as part of oral language and song as part of written language. We supplemented these activities by telling stories from the plots of Giti's books and from familiar life events such as "When Your Birthday Comes," as time and setting allowed.

The musical framework of any language is appropriated through a child's imitative babbling with phonemes set into larger intonation patterns. During this stage, a child in an English speaking environment learns to sound like an English speaking child; by nine months Giti sounded like an English speaking child. She had determined HOW PEOPLE SOUND WHEN THEY TALK. Moreover, she could play with her new ability. In conversations with her and when reading to her, she echoed what she heard. When the echoes intruded too much into the interaction and the participating adult became annoyed, she considered it a game of great fun. At 14 months she began to pick up her books, family magazines, or fourth class mail and practice book babbling. Visitors who saw her commented, "She sounds as if she is reading." Apparently she was separating a broad framework for HOW PEOPLE SOUND WHEN THEY READ as opposed to HOW PEOPLE SOUND WHEN THEY TALK.

Giti at 1 year had four labels comprehensive to English speakers: "baby" for herself, her human and animal toys, and other babies; "bye" and "hi" for the appropriate leaving and entering events; and "yeah" in response to questions. By 14 months she clearly and consistently divided her world into /baba/ to represent people, /dayday/ to represent animals, and the word "bird" for birds. Only twice did she fail to make these separations and she corrected the mislabeling in both instances. Giti applied these categories to her books and could use labeling in reading and oral language as mutually reinforcing activities. *The Little Golden Picture Dictionary* provided many animals and objects which were identified for her and matched with the real objects in the home whenever available. She also pointed to an object in her books, said /ə/ with rising intonation, and made eye contact when requesting its name. Using, "What's this?" adults could also question her for the names of the objects in her books or in the environment. Her vocabulary grew rapidly and she subdivided her categories of living beings and defined a category for labels of objects.

Making obvious associations dominated Giti's learning from the environment from 15 months on. Eye glasses would go with an eyeglass case, an empty cup would be matched with the refrigerator or the kitchen sink for a drink, and her jacket could only mean she was going out. She would become frantic if

I dared to leave the house without my pocketbook or her father without his briefcase. Objects could not be misplaced in any room and tantrums ensued if the order she was constructing varied from what she believed to be the only true patterns. She began to associate across books at 20 months. When "bunny" and the picture appeared in her dictionary, she would run to get *Pat the Bunny,* point at the bunny, and say "bunny." When the little dog Ted pulled his pockets inside out in *Big Dog and Little Dog* and the text read, "Ted was always broke," she would run to get *Mother Goose* and find Simple Simon who also pulled his pockets inside out to demonstrate his lack of funds. Once she found the appropriate picture in the second book, she would show it to us and say, "He broke."

Giti clearly distinguished print by 20 months. She continued to maintain her book babbling whenever she was not interested in labeling an item in a book or a magazine. She applied this activity to her books, our books, fourth class mail, credit cards, billboards, and license plates but never with a nonprint items. She consistently identified the broad yellow *M* as /onaw/ (for McDonald's) whether it stood alone or appeared on a billboard or cup. *M* was the first letter actually triggering a complete oral response. She would also respond /onaw/ (for McDonald's) to the same style of *M* written on paper. In the context of appropriate locations, from 22 months, she would say "Sears" when entering Sears and "Ayr Way" when entering or passing Ayr Way. Her sense of direction in finding the public swimming pool, the bank, a particular restaurant, and friends' houses was flawless. At 24 months, when the family stopped for a red light in an unfamiliar town, she shouted, "K-Mart!" The stores were so numerous that the marquee was not immediately obvious to us. Farther along the road, she noted "Ayr Way" and was also correct. At the next rest stop, when presented with *Kmart* printed as the logo by her father, she read, "Kmart." Until *ayr way* was written exactly as the logo she could not read it. Once the "A" was printed typographically and the tail of the "Y" swung to the left, she immediately read it and pointed to the space between the *ayr* and *way* and said, "Flower," directing us to put a flower rather than a hyphen between the words. Met with enthusiasm, she began to question, "That?" (rising intonation) and point from her car seat as she passed familiar places. Once the labels were provided, she recognized them again and again. The logos were cut out and glued on cards which were then punched and held together with yarn. She could practice reading these homemade books at will. By 26 months she could read 22 signs (see Appendix 4). The logos could be large or small or even partially missing. She would also run to get the newspaper to be able to read, or clap and shout the name when a familiar store or item was advertised on television. When grocery shopping, she could accurately handle such assignments as, "go and get a Bounty papertowel," or "Find a big box of Cheerios." She could also read her own name printed upper and lower case inside her books or on cards sent to her, and printed all upper case on name tags given at the public library storyhours.

By 24 months, she demonstrated labeling and associating within print. Pointing at the *K* in *Special K*, she would say, "Kmart," and pointing at the *m* in *Kmart*, she would say, "McDonald's." At 25 months, when encountering print, if she failed to read the logo correctly, usually because she was tired or disinterested, she supplied the name of its category. For instance, Kroger became "grocery" and Rice Krispies became "cereal." By 30 months, she demonstrated the *z* on her wooden block and said, "Look. Like in *zoo*." At this time she started to recognize large print whole words in her books. She learned to read "you" through the predictable ending of Sesame Street's Big Bird and Little Bird's *Big and Little Book*.

Big Bird: You know Little Bird, even though I like all those big things, I can think of one LITTLE thing that I like a whole lot.
Little Bird: Really? You know, I can think of one BIG thing that I really like too!
Both: YOU!

Not only could she supply "you" at the appropriate moment in the oral reading, but she could read YOU printed on paper. Dr. Seuss' more predictable *Marvin K. Mooney, Will You Please Go Now* provided practice with YOU and she learned to read GO and NOW in a variety of print contexts. In addition, she began to gain understandings from her books which she could even apply in the future. *500 Words to Grow On*, which she received as a member of "The Best Book Club Ever" from Random House, showed different kinds of boats. We had no occasion to differentiate within the category "boat" in conversation, but when Giti was confronted with real boats on a lake, she correctly classified them, "That sailboat. That motor boat."

Reading continued to grow as her favorite activity. Her

day centered on three major reading sessions: after waking; before an afternoon nap; before going to sleep at night. At one sitting, which lasted usually an hour, she requested the reading of five to ten books, which she selected 90 percent of the time. The remaining 10 percent represents occasions when we sought variety in what was to be read (see Appendix 5 for one month's selections made completely by Giti). Whenever a new book arrived from her book club or was purchased, she wanted first to look through it and then have it read to her. In her 28th month, there was not enough time available to satisfy her ever-increasing demands. We read three books at one sitting and then urged her to read herself. Now before the reading periods began, she confidently separated the books into those that she wanted others to read, and those familiar enough to her that she would read them herself. Rather than employing her previously useful book babbling, she labeled comprehensive people, objects, and actions in the sequence of the story. Only when she attempted totally unfamiliar print, such as the fourth class mail or one of our books, did she resort to book babbling. While storytelling, singing, and questioning were maintained primarily by the adults around her, she began to handle more of the reading activities herself. She would sit by her bookshelf and read by herself between the major interaction periods with adults. We frequently had to urge her into other activities to create a better-rounded day.

Giti's 28th month involved the entire family in what at the time appeared to be a crisis in communication. At the beginning of the month, her sentences were seven to ten words long and usually comprehensible to adults. However, during this month two changes in her conversation appeared. Gradually very little of what she said was intelligible and yet she seemed to be saying more and more. She was understood only if limited to two or three words at one time. By the beginning of her 30th month occasional words were distinguishable in her long tirades, and slowly by the end of the same month, she could once again be understood. She now told stories.

> When my birthday comes, we invite all my friends, Kate, Donna, Ziba, Sally, the babies. I have big cake with candles. I blow candles (demonstrates). Be careful. Then Mommy goes into bedroom. Shhh! (She holds forefinger to her mouth.) Surprise (she shouts). Out she comes with my new red tricycle. I be very happy. I be three.

Her reading had changed drastically as well. From labeling objects and events in the story sequence, she developed a complete story line. Her oral language structure had filled in significantly and her oral reading demonstrated more complex

---

Text

[Picture of barefoot Susie with her mother brushing her hair while she looks in mirror, followed by picture of Susie climbing rocks]

At the end of the summer Susie's mother said, "Tomorrow we are going back home to the city." So Susie went to say goodbye to her summer friends.

She went to the meadow. "Goodbye, Mr. Grasshopper," she said. "Would you like to come to the city with me?" "Oh, no!" said the grasshopper. "I couldn't jump on the city streets."

She went to the cow. "Goodbye, Mrs. Cow," said Susie. "Would you like to come to the city with me?" "Oh, no!" said the cow. "You don't have such green grass in the city."

She went to the duck. "Goodbye, little ducks," she said. "Would you like to come to the city with me?" "Oh, no!" quacked the ducks. "We live in the pond. We couldn't come to the city with you."

She went to the frog and the bunny rabbit...

and the birds and the flowers in the fields.

But no one, not even one, would go to the city with Susie.

Susie felt very sad. So she thought and thought and then she knew what she would do.

With her box of crayons on a big white paper, she drew her summer friends. She drew the grasshopper, the cow, the ducks, the frog, the bunny rabbit, the birds.

"Now," she said, "I will not forget my summer friends when I go home to the city."

And this is the picture that Susie drew.

---

[2]A predictable book presents a story which the reader may anticipate because of the familiar syntactic and semantic contexts.

Baghban

semantic intent as well. A comparative transcription of her reading of the moderately predictable [2] *Summer Friends* at 27 months and then again at 30 months demonstrates this growth.

27 months	30 months
Susie's mommy. Hair brush. No shoes.	Susie went to say goodbye to her friends.
Come. Oh no.	She went to the grasshopper. Would you like to come to the city with me? Oh, no, he said.
Cow. Oh no.	She went to the cow. Would you like to come to the city with me? Oh no, cow said.
Ducks. Oh no.	She went to the ducks. Would you like to come to the city with me? Oh no. No water.
Frog. Bunny.	She went to the frog and the bunny rabbit...
Birds. Flowers.	and the birds, and the flowers in the fields.
No. No.	No one. Not even one would come. So she thought and thought.
Crayons. Paper. Makes picture.	She takes her crayons and a big paper. She draws the grasshopper and the cow, and the birds, and the flowers, and the ducks.
Susie drawing.	Here is Susie's drawing.

A nonpredictable nonfiction book such as *The Little Duck* has a weak story line and more text. However, at 30 months rather than resorting to her book babbling or labeling objects and events in the text, with a story schema she could sample the text, predict what was to happen based on previous experience with the book, and confirm her understanding by pointing to the appropriate photos in the text on seven of the 29 pages.

Page	Text	Reading at 30 months
	From *The Little Duck* by Judy Dunn. Copyright by Random House, Inc. 1976. Reprinted by permission of the author and Random House, Inc.	
1	One morning in early spring a little boy was fishing in the pond near his farm. Again and again he threw out his line. The boy gathered his things to go home.	He was fishing. He threw it out again and again. He found it. A duck's egg.
	Suddenly he saw something nestled in the tall grass at the pond's edge. It was an egg—a duck's egg. The little boy carried the egg home with him.	
3	He placed the egg in an incubator so it would keep warm. Every day the boy turned the egg over as gently as a mother duck.	He took it home and put it in the incubator.
4	Finally, after twenty-eight days of waiting and watching, the boy heard something peeping and pecking inside the egg. The shell cracked...and broke open. Henry, the little duck was hatched.	Here comes Henry.
10	The boy was afraid he would catch cold. So he set the hairdryer on "warm" and dried Henry's feathers in no time.	He dried it.
12	When the little duck was dry again, he found a cozy resting place on the broad back of the family dog. Together they dozed in the sunshine.	He's on the doggie.
22	On weekends the boy stayed home. Then Henry was happy. He had a playmate and sometimes, on warm winter days when the boy was away, his grandfather would rock Henry on the porch.	And on the grandfather.
29	Soon Henry and his friend had an egg of their own, nestled in the tall grass beside the pond.	And the duck goes to make a chocolate egg.[3]

[3]Easter was approaching and she had been fascinated by the candy eggs in the stores.

A return to the beginning of *The Little Duck* at 33 months, contrasted with Giti's reading of the same text at 30 months, demonstrates an even greater ability to complete the structure of less-structured material.

Text	Reading at 33 months	Reading at 30 months
One morning in early spring a little boy was fishing in the pond near his farm. Again and again he threw out his line. The boy gathered his things to go home.	The little boy was fishing. Here is his fishing rod. (She points.) He threw it out again and again. He wanted to go home. In the grass he found an egg. It was a duck's egg. He took it home.	He was fishing. He threw it out again and again. He found it. A duck's egg.
Suddenly he saw something nestled in the tall grass at the pond's edge. It was an egg—a duck's egg. The little boy carried the egg home with him.		

A little book of photos whose text is Walt Whitman's poem, "I Hear America Singing," permitted minimal use of Giti's experiential background. She found the book on her parents' bookshelf and had not heard the poem previously. However, rather than resorting to book babbling or labeling the text in sequence, in this extremely difficult reading situation, she struggled to construct an oral reading with some kind of semantic intent.

Reading at 30 months

I hear 'merica singing. (She asked, "What does this say?" and repeated the title.)
He has his boots on.
The flamingoes have long legs.
The umbrella is over here.
Peter and the Wolf scares me.

Speculations

Ethnography has been defined as an attempt to describe the methods people use to get along in the social world (McDermott, 1977). When we try to describe how people talk to each other in everyday life or the ethnography of speaking, we move beyond the language itself to the relations between the people involved in the conversation and the context in which the conversation is taking place. In this sense, it is not so much verbal ability that the participants use and learn as it is communicative competence. When caregivers look at and talk to newborns who cannot possibly understand them, they indicate that eye contact and speech provide the means to ensure individual survival and fulfillment of basic needs. In fact, if we view humankind as possessing a language acquisition ability, we may consider such ability within the continuum of each individual's life. As infants, we unconsciously select to model speech over noise and persist in conquering its intricacies; as untrained caregivers, we initiate, modify, maintain, and upgrade informative dialogue. When the infant and caregiver communicate, they want to communicate more. The speech act is self-reinforcing.

Giti began to communicate to survive and in order to maintain herself she needed some control over her environment. Dialogue not only offered her a vehicle to gain control but a means to participate in life itself. In return, dialogue required that she learn to play a role in the conversation. She noted that one partner gives the other a message; the other's speech is influenced by the first, and the initiator's subsequent speech is influenced by the response elicited. One person talks at a time and each person's contribution is related to what has been said and what the larger situation may be. Ideally, the cooperation of the participants must be maintained throughout this interaction. However, the interaction may really depend on what the participants are trying to establish as their relationship. Initially the formal structures of language are encountered through the joint attention-joint activity of the caregiver and child in the contexts of work and play (Bruner, 1975c). Yet this informal situation is educational. The interaction requires the caregiver to provide information and direct experiences and requires the child to learn. And the linguistic information is necessarily bound to the context in which it is learned. In this way, children become participating members of the social group that uses their particular language.

As the child of professional parents, Giti was exposed to a rich print environment. Reading to a child can also be considered an ordered interaction between child and caregiver set in a context of mutual activity. Giti's oral language developed out of necessity first and as play later, but her reading developed as play in the sense of "child's work" from the beginning. The social relation motivated the reading. She was, however, ready and able to apply what she had already learned about human interaction and oral language to the reading act. In fact a dialogue schema may be a prerequisite for learning from early interaction (recall Appendix 3 for Giti's interaction with me). Like Richard in the following example, she transferred assumptions from her experiences with oral diaglogue to the more focused situation of print.

> In this instance Richard and his mother are "reading" the pictures in a book. Before this kind of learning begins, certain things have already been established. Richard has learned about pointing as a pure indicating act, marking usual or unexpected objects rather than things wanted immediately. He has also learned to understand that sounds refer in some singular way to objects or events. Richard and his mother, moreover, have long since established well-regulated turn-taking routines, which probably were developing as early as his third or fourth month. And finally, Richard has learned that books are to be looked at, not eaten or torn; that objects depicted are to be responded to in a particular way with sounds in a pattern or dialogue. (Bruner, 1978, p. 44)

Early reading is also an oral dialogue that teaches. Pines (1979, p. 35) presents another child.

> "What's that?" asks the mother, pointing to a page in a picture book. "Bow-Wow," replies the 18 month old boy. "Good," says the mother, and she points to the picture on the following page. "What's that?" she asks again, but in a different tone—with a rising inflection—for she knows that her child hasn't seen this animal before. And without waiting for his response, she answers for him: "A zebra." It sounds as if this mother is teaching her child vocabulary, and she is. But she is also doing something far more important and basic: She is teaching him the rules of dialogue in human society. Through such exchanges he learns to recognize the meaning of different intonations, to respond to questions, to take turns. (Pines, 1979, p. 35)

And because Giti had similar experiences in an English print environment with literate caregivers, by 18 months she had learned to turn a book rightside up and turn pages from left to right. About print, she learned with more experience that books tell a story and pictures support the story; we look at print from left to right, top to bottom; and the print seems to trigger oral language that she can recognize and even reproduce to some degree.

The introduction of *Pat the Bunny,* as a predictable book requiring participation on Giti's part at 9 months, upholds the joint attention/joint activity core of the speech act. One page of text was read to her followed by the appropriate action as a response. After just one reading of the text and demonstration of the necessary action, she was able to carry out her role in the interaction. As Shatz (1978) indicates, when children do not have the necessary linguistic structures or vocabulary to maintain dialogue, they resort to action to continue the communication. Similarly, adults frequently can be seen using facial expressions and gestures, not so much as a substitute but rather as an accompaniment to oral language. Thus, *Pat the Bunny* introduced Giti to reading through a strategy with which she was already familiar in the broader contexts of oral language.

The associate hypothesis that the dialogue is initially controlled by the caregiver and dependent on a continually revised understanding of the child's competence can be demonstrated in oral language and reading development. In both cases, I, as any other caregiver, initially limited my speech and maintained regular word order. Both oral language and reading interactions involved, "Look," to get Giti's attention and to command her attention to some object in the environment or text. Yes/No questions prompted communication both in the daily order of events ("Are you thirsty?") and in the texts ("Do you see the dog?"). Observations or comments provided opportunities to share emotional rather than purely linguistic reactions about events in life ("Look at the rain!") or in the texts ("What a silly cat!"). Every response in behavior and oral language was positively reinforced in all situations. As Giti grew to label, my questions in the larger environment and in reading changed to "What's this?" which required information rather than agreement or disagreement. However, Yes/No responses were still required to help labeling ("Is this a tree?). When she could handle labeling accurately, more overt effort was demanded of her in both conversation and reading. She was held accountable for information which I felt she could supply. As places and prepositions were added to her vocabulary, *WH*-questions were gradually added to the dialogue ("Where is the ball?"). Definition kinds of questions were continued, but with the element of choice involved (Is this a tree or a flower?"). By 24 months, Giti had grown into assuming responsibility for maintenance of the dialogue through her own participation with language, and by 28 months she was confident enough to assume responsibility for reading familiar materials. Child-caregiver roles in both oral language and reading achieved more balance.

Giti used oral language and reading as mutually reinforcing processes. Initially, oral language strongly supported reading activities. Rhymes from *Mother Goose* which were sung and the retelling of shared experiences from daily life and from books were enjoyed at any time and in any place. The freedom and pleasure found in singing and storytelling as elements of oral language development were transferred to the more restrictive setting of encounters with print. Very early Giti recognized through pictorial clues which *Mother Goose* pages contained songs she knew. She participated by clapping and attempting to sing when she heard the song or the text read. By 14 months oral language and written language appeared to be mutually reinforcing. She was able to label parts of her environment and could use her dictionary to make associations from which she could generalize. By 26 months, in some instances, written language could even expand oral language growth. Categorizing "boats" into "sailboats" and "motor boats" demonstrated that she had indeed learned about the world through her books. The functional value of her concepts was ready to be demonstrated whenever the form might be needed. Reading had provided knowledge through indirect experience.

Schema theory in its broadest sense suggests an appropriate means of analyzing the transition exemplified by Giti at 28 months. At nine months she babbled like a child speaking English and at 14 months she babbled like a child reading English. Once these intonation schemata or skeletons were formed, she began to fill them in with words and sentences. Apparently in this 28th month some breathing space was needed to assimilate her learning. Her seven to ten word sentences, which were usually comprehensible to adults, and her reading which consisted of appropriate identifications in the sequence of the story, led to the separation of one schema for storytelling and one schema for the idea that "books talk in a special way." The 30th month telling of "when My Birthday Comes" and the 30th month reading of *Summer Friends* demonstrate a complete story line, i.e. a beginning, a middle, and an ending. By backing away for more than one month, the separation and formation of the two processes clicked. At 30 months, even when presented with less predictable material, such as *The Little Duck,* Giti attempted strategies to assimilate what she knew about the content of the text into her schema of how a book should talk. Interestingly, adults often forget that the ease with which we tackle reading materials depends on the extent to which the materials match our previous experiences and our language. The closer the match, the greater our success as readers. Each of us becomes a poor reader when needing to understand a law brief or tax form, or a good reader with a Harlequin Romance. The use of predictable books promotes successful literacy by matching knowledge of the world through oral language to written. Faced with Whitman's "I Hear America Singing," Giti rightfully could do very little.

Giti's oral language and reading developed in an interrelated sequence of stages. As Table 1 indicates, Giti's reading production began only five months behind her oral language development. Both oral language and reading development reached a plateau in the 30th month with the separation and formation of a more specific schema for each process. The time span in months from the onset of babbling in oral language to the storytelling schema was 21 months, while the time span from the onset of book babbling to the story reading schema was 16 months. Although Giti began her association with reading later, she apparently learned faster because she could build on an ever-expanding oral language base as well as her physiological and cognitive maturation. Oral language, which had satisfied early, immediate needs, became fun as well through songs, rhymes, and storytelling. Early reading fun, in which she could participate through action supplemented by oral language, evolved into satisfying needs as well. From HOW PEOPLE SOUND WHEN THEY READ at 14 months, she determined HOW BOOKS TALK IN A SPECIAL WAY at

Table 1
Chronological Comparison of Oral Language
and Reading Development

Approximate Age in Months	Oral Language	Approximate Age in Months	Reading
9	babbling	9	first encounter with a book
12	labeling in environment		
		14	book babbling
		14	labeling in books
15	associations in environment		
20	categorizations in environment	20	associations across books
24	assumption of equal role in conversation		
		25	categorization of print items
		28	assumption of responsibility in reading
30	storytelling schema	30	story reading schema

30 months. She continues to refine her evolving definition of how reading functions in her life as her language and cognitive development continue and her experiences broaden.

Since Giti's activities have been considered reading, we may ask, "Just when did she begin to read?" An example of intrinsic motivation to read is described by Block.

> Peter loved books as soon as he could handle them. He would sit on the floor and ritualistically take books from the shelves, open them, turn pages, close them, replace them and examine others. Once he said to me, "Words, words, words." (Block, 1972, p. 58)

And it follows that if the books interest him, Peter will almost certainly ask questions about the words. According to Ryan (1977, p. 159), "When a child responds to a common symbol around the house, beginning reading should be considered to be occurring." Then Giti began to read when she recognized *M* for /onaw/ (McDonald's) and *Kmart* in context. Or was it when she identified the *m* in *Kmart* only from print? Yet she was also reading when she determined that a book talks in a special way. Many preschoolers will read you a book by looking at its pictures or while looking over the top of the book, and supply words you dare to skip as you read familiar stories. In fact, these events observed by so many parents strongly emphasize the need to revise our definition of reading to include notions of development. If 3-year-olds exposed to print exhibit similar characteristics and consider themselves to be reading, and 4 year olds exposed to print exhibit similar characteristics and consider themselves to be reading, then so should we.

An even more difficult question may be, "When was the onset of readiness to read?" According to Gibson and Levin (1975, p. 265), given children's natural curiosity, they should be considered ready to extract information from the printed page as soon as they have the opportunity to look at any book. Thus, Giti, who received her very own real book at 9 months, is reading. If she does with print what other children about her age exposed to print do with print, then she *is* reading. "Readiness *for* reading" becomes, therefore, an irrelevant concept.

Table 2 summarizes Giti's oral language and reading development in the first 3 years of her life. Her success with dialogue as a vehicle for handling her early environment led naturally to the use of interaction as an approach to early reading. Realizing the value of her play with reading for communication, she applied her oral language learning strategies to the reading situation. As physiological and cognitive development advanced and her strategies became more complex, she subdivided her broad linguistic framework into two schemata useful to her life: one for oral language contexts and one for written language contexts.

In summary, the speech act with interactions manipulated by the caregiver fits the early action-dialogue contexts examined. Table 2 indicates that as an outgrowth of dialogue, the child continues to test hypotheses in order to refine schemata which in turn continue to influence her information-processing strategies and her oral language interactions.

A speech act approach integrates non-literary and literary discourse into one basic model for communicative activities (Pratt, 1977). With ordinary conversation, the

Table 2
Process Model of the Development of Storytelling and Story Reading Schemata

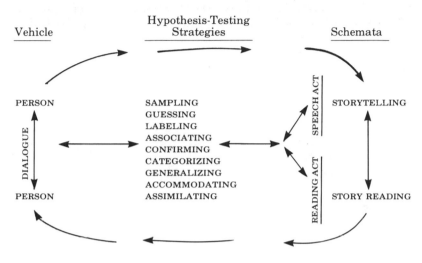

speaker and listener are physically present in a shared context. Comprehension may be aided by the total situation as well as participants' nonverbal cues. Each person takes a turn playing initiator or audience. The aspects of dialogue are obvious. In literary discourse, a writer may be immediately faced with a blank page, but an eventual audience is assumed (Graves, 1979), and a reader uses personal experience to understand the intent of even a noncontemporary writer. The writing itself is the shared context.

Giti's oral and written language schemata grew out of her participation in dialogue. The schemata in turn aided her understanding of further oral language interactions. She learned to handle the characteristics of linguistic structures for specific nonliterary and literary contexts. Giti's storytelling, story reading, and conversational abilities are interrelated, intersupportive linguistic modes of the same communicative model. Such a model is required not only for her survival, but also for her development. Provided the broad schemata continue to have meaning in her life, they are refined and influence her communicative competence. Semantic intent has been and remains her earliest and most basic learning strategy. Through language she is constructing a social reality (Halliday, 1975b) which she can understand and in which she can find her place.

Written Language and Drawing

Observations

We frequently wrote in front of Giti. Messages were written down while talking on the telephone. Grocery lists were written on small pieces of paper. Thank you notes were composed after receiving gifts, and cards were mailed when gifts were sent or holidays occurred. Checks were signed and forms completed. She began to approach whenever I might be writing and stand at my elbow to watch. If Baba was sitting on the couch writing, she would crawl up and sit next to him, peeping over his shoulder and leaning hard on his arm. By 17 months, she attempted to grab pens and paper when we tried to write and she would shout, "Me," or/papa/for either or both the paper and pen. With only a few demonstrations of how to hold the pen and fit her fingers around it, she began to scribble on sheets of scrap paper which she could remove as she wanted from a drawer kept especially for her. Pens were located in a holder at the telephone or in a desk drawer, both places she could reach when she wanted to initiate writing. She would also remove pens from pockets and pocketbooks and compete with us for the use of pens when we started to write. Putting a sheet of paper on a magazine and then on her lap, she would practice writing while sitting next to us. She would also lie on her stomach on the floor and practice on her own or command one of us to join her. Her attempts at written language were met with, "That's good," "How nice," or "Just fine." A small notebook was carried outside the house in my pocketbook to occupy Giti in restaurants or while waiting for appointments. Figure 1 (18 months) is one of many examples which demonstrates Giti's delight in filling up whole pages of her notebook.

Figure 1. 18 Months

When questioned, "What did you write?" or "What did you draw?" she pointed to what she had done or banged on it with her whole hand. When asked, "Please write something for me," or "Please draw something for me," she would use the implements that were most handy and do the same kind of scribbling. Occasionally she would be presented with crayons at friends' houses or in certain restaurants, but she seemed reluctant to use them. When given her own box of crayons at home with a drawing demonstration, she broke them and selected ballpoint or felt-tipped pens for use instead. We did not

Baghban

Figure 2. 19 Months

allow her to use pencils because of the hazards of sharp points. Introduction of a magic slate also proved inadequate for recording her written samples since Giti would lift the top layer before a flash photo could be taken or the photos that were taken were not very clear. Giti's grandparents visited during this month and frequently drew pictures to entertain her, while we remained preoccupied with writing. By 19 months (Figure 2), her scribbling did not sprawl over the page to such an extent, and she appeared to have noticed dots in others' writings which she reproduced in this sample as well as several others.

Figure 3.   20 Months

At 20 months (Figure 3) she concentrated on circles as the major items on her paper, with or without dots, and with isolated smaller circles or wavy lines separated from the larger circles or placed within them.

She often attempted to write as soon as possible after watching an adult write. In this case, her productions more resembled English script than the productions she might achieve independently during the same period. Figure 4 (20 months) shows her reproduction right after watching Baba write a paragraph in English and while sitting next to him on the couch.

Figure 4. 20 Months

Figure 5.   21 Months

One of her favorite play activities at 21 months was writing on print. She would attack the fourth class mail, newspapers, and flyers just to scribble on the writing. If one side of an advertisement was blank, she would turn it to the side with the writing and scribble all over it. Her notebook at 21 months (Figure 5) demonstrates continued practice with circles and some of linearity.

Figure 6. 22 Months

When requested, "Please write for me," or "Please draw for me," she made circles freely. Once when asked, "What did you write?" she pointed to the mass of circles she had produced and said, "Snoopy." On another occasion she pointed to another set of circles she had produced and said, "Cat." When asked, "What did you draw?" she did not respond. By 22 months (Figure 6), her circles were occasionally incorporated into a linear expansion. She could also use her crayons.

At 23 months (Figure 7) she continued to scribble on print and practice her own writing separately but on the same paper. Her writing sessions now averaged 10 minutes at a time. By 24 months she spontaneously began to practice book babbling on her own writing. The day she looked at the *Kmart* logo on a

Figure 7. 23 Months

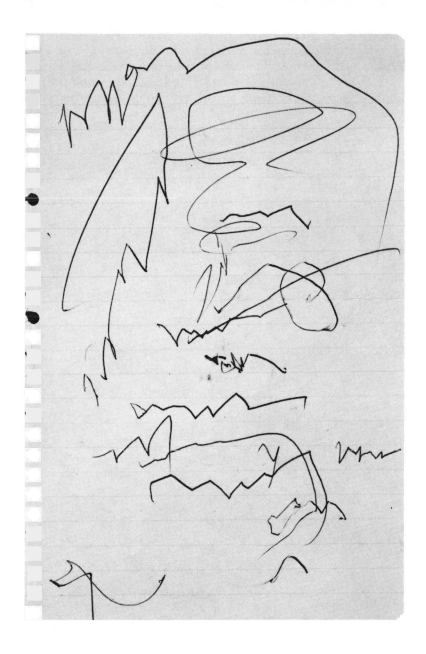

Figure 8.   24 Months

card, pointing to the *m* and saying, "onalds," she attempted *m* in her writing (Figure 8). After completing a row of peaks, she began another row and said, "Marce," associating *m* with my name as well. The activities coincided with the time that she began to read signs aloud in her environment and alone as logos.

Figure 9.   25 Months

Baghban

For her second birthday she received a puzzle of her name cut into wood and would now more frequently order us, "Write /diydiy/." At 25 months she started to write G from the bottom to the top, point to what she had done, and say /diydiy/ for her own name, Giti. Enraptured by the representation, she practiced G in isolation (Figure 9) on masses of paper. She could also contrast and label her G with "onald" (Figure 10).

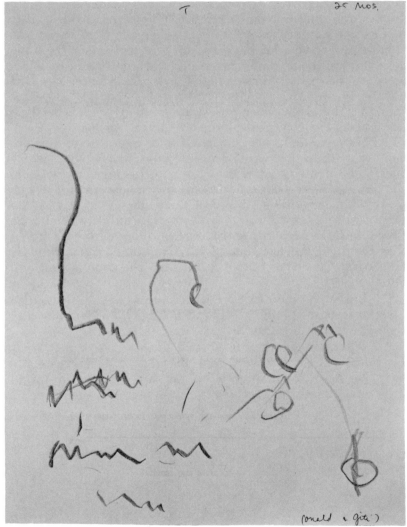

Figure 10.   25 Months

She labeled small circles "apple" or "flower," but when asked to draw a picture she did not respond.

If asked to write "onald," she made her rows of peaks and if asked to write "Giti" she made her bottom to top *G*. Her grandparents visited when she was 26 months old and brought her a pegboard desk. Now with a place for her writing materials, she removed some of the paper from her supply drawer and placed it on the righthand side of the desk tray. After some adult prompting about other items that might be kept within, she put her crayons and pens on the left side of the desk tray. In the next months, friends gave her a small plastic box with tiny pencils and I bought her a pen on a necklace. Giti put the writing and drawing implements in her desk. Even at the end of this study, she neither puts small toys inside her desk nor forgets to close the desk top when she finishes.

Her grandparents continued to draw for her entertainment more than they wrote words. While Giti could not clearly distinguish drawing from writing among her own productions, she would always ask grandparents to draw for her and ask us to write for her. She scribbled at this time and said, "I write bunny," or "I draw bunny" with no discernible difference in the product. In her writing (Figure 11) she practices *G*s and in this instance labeled them Giti, Grandma, and Grandpa, perceiving that each name began with the same sound and letter.

Larger versions (Figure 12) with less discernible *G*s also appeared, possibly suggesting drawings of Grandma and Grandpa which began with *G* at the center.

After her grandparents' visit, Giti would ask me, "Write *Grandma*." If I wrote *Grandma*, Giti would become upset and say, "No, no. Draw Grandma." If she said, "Draw cup," and I drew a cup, she would start to cry and shout, "Write, write *cup*."

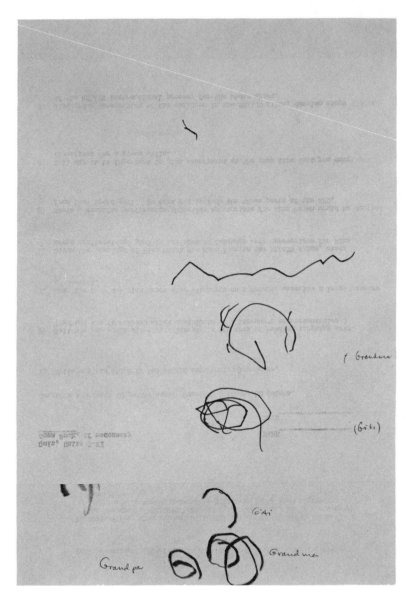

Figure 11. 26 Months

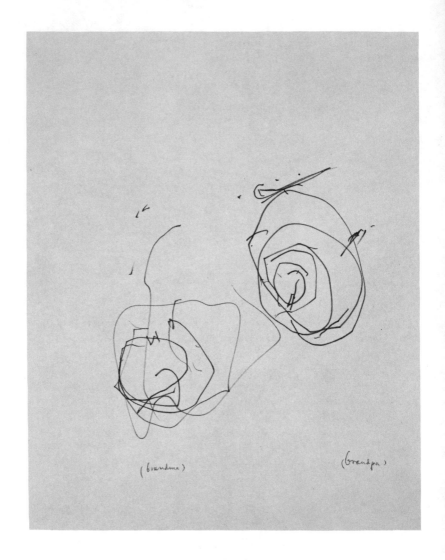

(grandma)　　　　　　　　　　　(grandpa)

Figure 12. 26 Months

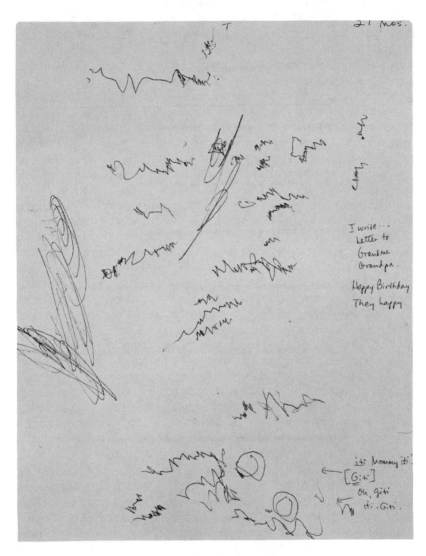

Figure 13. 27 Months

Her writing sessions were still 10 minutes long, but with frustration for both Giti and me while she attempted to sort out how to communicate what she wanted to appear on paper. At 27 months she began to organize her demands into dictations. She would give either of us a sheet of paper at home or hand one of us her notebook when out and order, "Write *Connie*." When that was accomplished, she continued, "Write *mall*" and so on through family names, her friends, and favorite places in town. These sessions began to last as long as 20 minutes with long pauses after each entry while she sat silently and studied the word. On her own, she began to compose letters in her notebook or on pieces of paper that she would occasionally fold over and announce, "I write Donna and Zibi a letter." Figure 13 (27 months) represents a long letter to her grandparents which she declared would make them happy. She also said, "Happy Birthday," apparently associating a recent birthday party for one of her friends with correspondence she received from her grandparents at the time of her own birthday.

At the bottom of the figure, her circles represent *Giti* and her linear expansions denote *Mommy* which she labeled herself. However, she kept trying to spell her name i, t, i, probably because so many people asked her, "What's your name?" and either she responded /diydiy/ or I responded, Giti. The questioner then usually asked, "How do you spell that?" so Giti had frequent opportunities to hear her name spelled aloud. *Baghban* is also difficult to communicate to native speakers of English and often is spelled in the course of a day. Periodically, Giti would singsong *b, a, b, a* which resulted from this spelling out situation and which she would practice while writing and extend to reading the family name on the door or mailbox. During this period she wrote on everything she could find, such as order blanks at the Sears catalog counter, forms at the post office, and checkout slips at the library, always on the side that had lines which needed to be completed. Rather than writing on the written language, she started to aim for the spaces between the lines for her own writing. She was not allowed to write on herself, on walls, or in her books. These rules were determined after one experience with each context and she did not repeat the episodes. Because we emphasized, "Get paper," "Write on paper," she searched out forms on which to scribble and paper placemats, napkins, and plates. The fourth class mail was always hers to open, to read, and to write on. She was now allowed pencils, colored markers, a fountain pen, chalk, and water colors.

Returning from a snack at the Big Wheel Restaurant in her 28th month, Giti took a small pad from the telephone stand and a pencil, stood in front of me with the pencil poised over the pad as the waitress in Big Wheel had done, and said, "You want" (rising intonation). I dictated, "Hot dog," then paused, "French fries," then paused, "Ice cream," which were all foods that Giti knew. Giti turned the page and more orders were dictated. Each time she made one linear expansion for each item ordered (Figure 14).

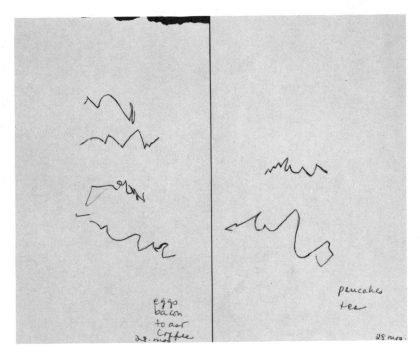

Figure 14. 28 Months

After 20 minutes, she said, "Free?" and "Ready?" indicating respectively a desire for the check and mutual agreement to leave, as well as the end of the game. During this same month she labeled her circular figures with parts that should mean a drawing of a person rather than writing symbols. For instance in Figure 15, she pointed to the uppermost circle and said, "Here are de eyes, de nose, de mouf." On the next piece of paper she drew a circle with marks on it and announced "Zibi," one of her friend's names.

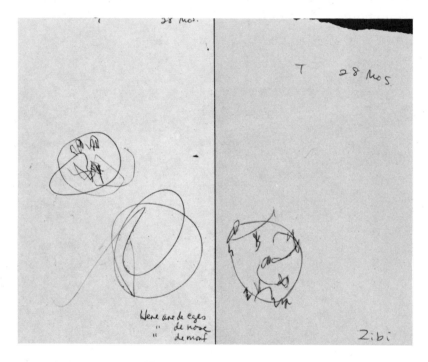

Figure 15. 28 Months

Baghban

If asked to draw Zibi, she responded, "You draw," and pushed paper and pen at either of us. Occasionally she did label what she was doing as drawing, but except for these two examples her productions scarcely resembled any people or objects she named. However, her visual memory and perception of detail were more subtle than frequently realized. Returning from a visit to a neighbor's, Giti sat at her desk and attempted to reproduce a desk calendar she had seen (Figure 16). She used an orange crayon in the upper righthand corner where the photograph of a flower had been and, although she used linear expansions for the days and weeks, she sang "2, 9, 6, 4, 3," while writing, which demonstrated that she had indeed noticed the numbers in the boxes on the calendar.

Figure 16. 28 Months

By 29 months, her dictations were frequently 25 words and could last as long as a half hour. Later, she would practice circles and her left to right linear expansions on her own while reviewing the previously dictated words in a sing-song. Her favorite letter *G* appeared more and more in what she now called writing (Figure 17).

Figure 17. 29 Months

When asked, "Can you write McDonald's?" she responded, "Yeah," and made a linear expansion (Figure 18). When asked "Can you write *Giti*?" and "Can you write *Grandma*?" on the same page, she worked from the bottom to the top making *G* and wrote symbols after each which demonstrated that she noted differences in word length for Giti, and for Grandma (recall Figure 11 when she wrote only *G* for each name).

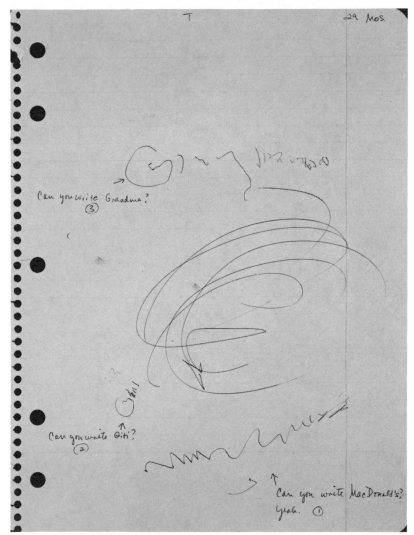

Figure 18. 29 Months

While she continued to confuse writing and drawing in her oral language, an adult observer could note differences in her activities. Figures 17 and 18 could be labeled "writing" because they demonstrate more control. However, Figure 19 may be labeled "drawing" because her body language indicated she was more relaxed in its creation, and the product's organization is also more relaxed.

Figure 19. 29 Months

Baghban

Her waitress game, after an overnight trip, became more complex. She would not only begin with, "You want," (rising intonation), and take orders, but she would now go to the window sill, stand and wait looking out the window, and then return with invisible items on her arms. The routine would be repeated as the orders were filled. The end of the game was still signaled by "Free" or "Money?" and the session could last as long as a half hour.

At 30 months, she wrote her name by itself on a piece of paper (Figure 20). The basic structure of the *G* appears written as usual from bottom to top followed by the upside down tent as a version of the joint at the finish of the *G*. The next three lines were typical of her name writing at this time. She usually had three vertical lines and some dots or dashes, probably parts of an *i* or *t,* we wrote her name in upper and lowercase letters.

Figure 20.   30 Months

When asked to draw, she continued to tell the questioner to draw. However, she managed some traces which she accompanied with oral language that indicated she was drawing, "Here's a wall, and a pond. Flower." (Figure 21).

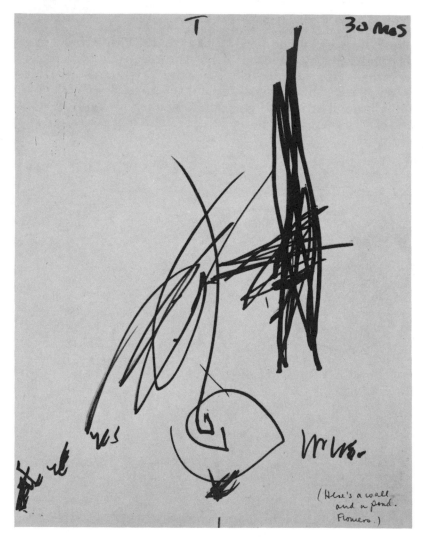

Figure 21.   30 Months

At the end of this month her letter writing is represented by a freer form as well. Her letters to her friend Bill, the custodian of her apartment building, are typical of her letters to everyone at this time (Figure 22).

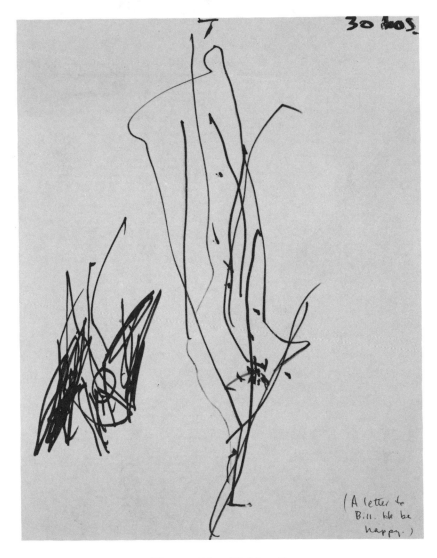

Figure 22. 30 Months

Figure 23. 31 Months

Rather than her previously used linear expansions for letters, she now seemed to be drawing her letters to people.

At 31 months, her grandparents came to visit and spent play periods drawing and writing whatever she wanted. Her drawing ability progressed measurably. Figure 23 demonstrates her versions of the three large snowmen in diagonal formation drawn by adults. Although on the back of a paper placemat, her six copies surround the three originals and are obvious enough to be located and identified.

She began to use, "I draw one," or "I drawing," with her creations. By 32 months she clearly distinguished her drawing of Baba (Figure 24) from her writing on a loan application which was on the back of a saleslip (Figure 25).

Figure 24.   32 Months

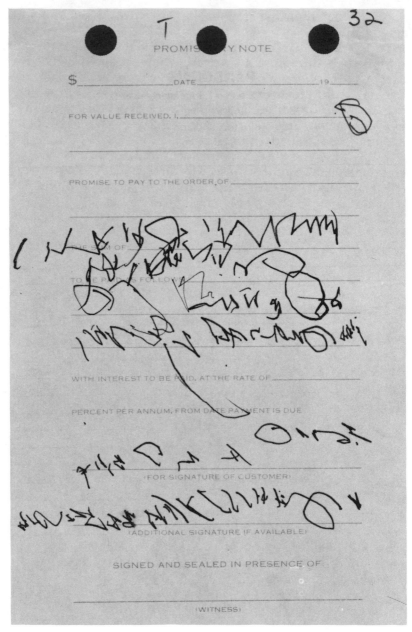

Figure 25. 32 Months

Baghban

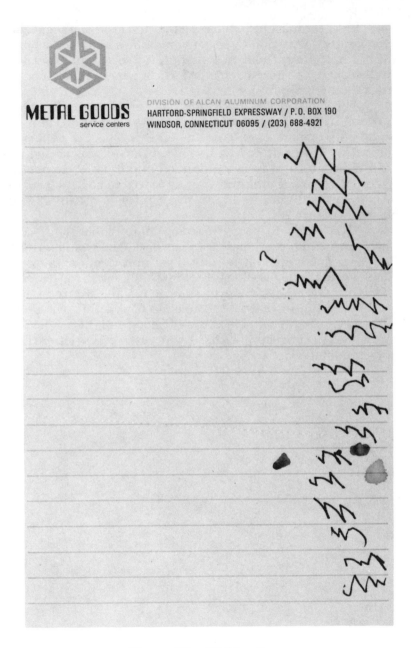

Figure 26. 32 Months

She continued her waitress game and after one suggestion from adults, "Why don't you get your babies and play school," she began to play school. Setting her stuffed animals and dolls on the couch, she gave each one a slip of paper, a tiny pencil, a cracker, and a sip from her plastic cup.

Then she began, "O.K. children, here we are today. Good cracker? Juice? You be happy. Now we writing." Then she would do a few linear expansions on each sheet of paper and end with, "That's all today. Bye bye." During this period, her writing began to go from right to left and from top to bottom. She would practice making what appeared to be lists from top to bottom beginning as far to the right side of the page as possible (Figure 26).

Her letters to people became more elaborate. Taking index cards and envelopes from our desk, she would write on the card, put it inside the envelope, and then write on the closure side of the envelope. Figure 27 is a letter to Grandma from Giti. Grandma is written on the inside card and Giti is written on the envelope, the reverse of real life where the addressee is on the outside of the envelope and the sender is in the inside but consistent with the way Giti receives letters from her grandmother.

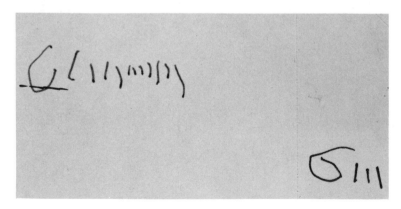

Figure 27. 32 Months

She continued to write letters to everyone she knew and to announce, "For Grandma," or "I write letters to Zibi." By 33 months she insisted on "mailing" them by taping them to her bedroom door or requiring parents to punch holes in the corner of each envelope and to tie a string to the envelope so she could drag her letters around like our mailman dragging his mail sack by the leather strap into the apartment building. Occasionally these letters would also be taped to her bedroom door with the string. While Giti used whatever paper or materials were available to her, including lined and graph paper, this month she took note of the lines and began to underline everything she wrote including her letters (Figure 28).

Figure 28. 33 Months

She continued to write from top to bottom, right to left (Figure 29).

Figure 29.   33 Months

She could fill in forms neatly (Figure 30).

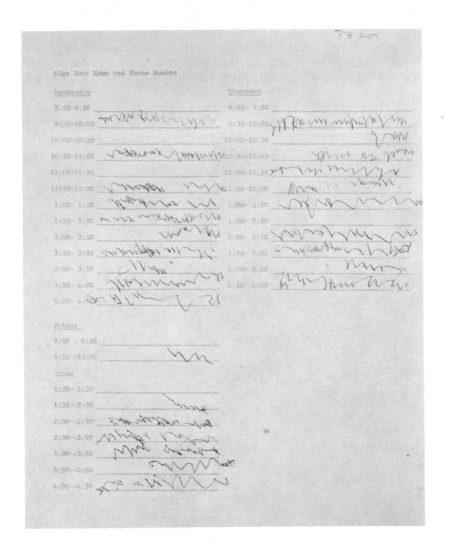

Figure 30. 33 Months

Waitressing and school were deserted at this time and letter writing and mailing her letters took up much of her writing play. She was only occasionally interested in large sheets of paper and then merely to staple them into a letter. She no longer cared to write in her notebook when outside. Always sociable and curious, her interest in other children and the world dominated her daily life more and more. She wrote her letters off and on all day, but not for long periods of time.

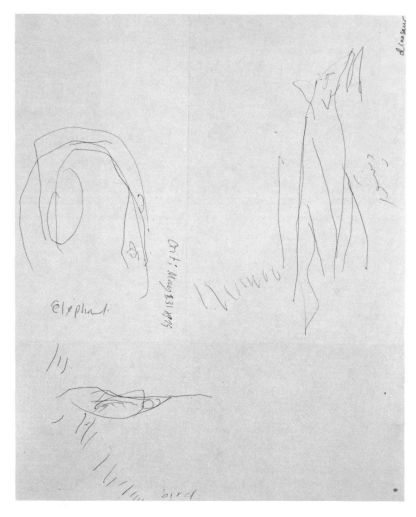

Figure 31. 33 Months

During this same month, her drawings began to look more like what she called them. Figure 31 represents respectively an elephant, a dinosaur, and a bird, and even from an adult point of view resembles these creatures in size or motion.

In her 34th month, her writing began again to go from left to right and return from the edge of the paper. She also continued to write from the top to the bottom of the sheet and to underline (Figure 32).

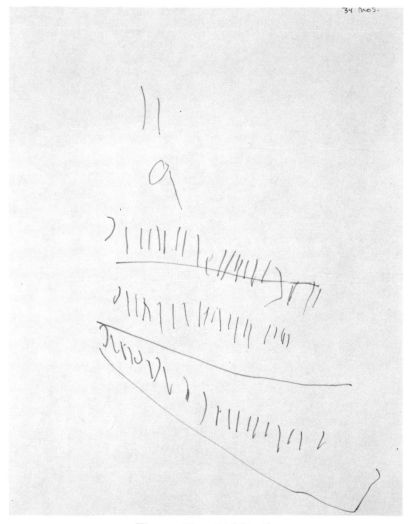

Figure 32.   34 Months

She had become confident enough in her understandings of drawing and writing to present both on the same page. Figure 33 shows a drawing of Grandma on the left and the title of her drawing, "Grandma," to the right.

Figure 33. 34 Months

Speculations

Just as Giti's oral language and early reading began in an interactive setting with a proficient user of language, so did her act of writing. Unlike her oral language, which developed out of necessity, her written language like her reading began as play-work activity. However, unlike her reading, we did not introduce her to writing by writing for her or to her. We wrote in front of her as part of our daily life obligations, and paper and pens were easily available. Giti's curiosity led her to the discovery of implements that left traces on paper which in turn motivated her to try to do what she saw us doing. But she needed us to show her what she needed to do. From us she learned how to hold a pen and on which materials it was possible to write. While she could practice alone, she continued to need a model if she wanted to learn to write. The sociocentric nature of her oral language learning and early reading applied to her beginning writing as well. The joint attention—joint activity of a parent sitting on the couch next to Giti or lying on the floor by her side writing and talking about writing supported Giti's fascination with the process of producing written language. Busy creating, Giti scarcely glanced at what she produced. She consumed piles of paper. Having lost interest in the sheets once she marked them, she scattered papers everywhere. Researchers in drawing (Morris, 1962; Van der Horst, 1950) have emphasized that for the young child, the act of drawing rather than the product is important. By extension, motor, kinesthetic, and affective rewards are significant aspects to young writers as well. Judging by the reams of paper Giti used, she demonstrated that she was no exception in her concern for process.

By 24 months, through her reproduction of peaks for the McDonald's arches, she made a written correction with a visual symbol she could read *m* and a sound she could produce /m/. Her product had meaning in her larger world and she began to conform more clearly to specific aspects of written language. With her spontaneous letter-writing to friends (27 months), Giti moved into an understanding of how her products could function in human relations wider than her family life. Her waitress game, begun at 28 months and expanded at 29 months, represents her further categorizations of the interactive functions of written language. At 31 months, though she had never spent a day in school, she began a game of teaching school with writing as part of her curriculum. Undoubtedly having parents who were somehow "in school" and frequently writing allowed this connection, as well as children's television and books about going to school. A big event of dreary winter days was a trip to the lobby of the apartment building to play with other children while the mailman sorted the mail. The family's fourth class mail belonged to Giti to do with as she wished and grandparents sent her cards and notes. By the end of her 31st month, letter writing succeeded all writing activities as her favorite. The products she created were kept with tape on her bedroom door or issued to her mother with, "You save dis." Written language was definitely valued communication for her. From communicating about written language at 18 months, she could now engage in interaction conducted only in writing.

As with Giti's oral language and early reading, the dialogue was initially controlled by the caregiver. Unlike oral language, the very early context of written language does not always prompt a topic for communication, and unlike reading, there is no prop such as a book to direct the interaction. The only props are the implements with which one can write. For these reasons, the caregiver must constantly impose a context for the written language during the interaction. Simultaneously, the learner must deal creatively with the message while attempting to conform to a system of symbols. This doublesided creativity brings difficulty both in maintenance and control of the interaction and in the evaluation of the child's ever changing competence. However, while perhaps less obvious than in the development of oral language and reading, the tenets of the speech act approach are evidenced in the development of written language.

Like oral language, dialogue with written language was initially difficult to sustain and consisted of a great deal of acting both on our part and on Giti's part. I would begin, "Let me show you how to write *Giti*," and write it down. Giti would bang on whatever I wrote or imitate whatever I did to communicate her interest in continuing the interaction. We always responded positively, which maintained the situation, and then attempted another example. When Giti could produce on her own, we would question, "What did you write?" or

"What did you draw?" or command, "Please write for me," "Please draw for me," or "Let's write." These were primarily the questions and commands throughout much of Giti's written language development, since writing did not prompt the variety of questions and commands found in oral language and reading contexts. Observations on her products also tended to be more general, usually forms of positive reinforcement such as, "That's good," or "Fine." Once she began to write McDonald's (24 months), Giti (25 months), and Grandma (26 months), there was something more specific on which to comment, "That looks like Giti. I can read it." Questions could also be aimed at what she could write, "Can you write McDonald's?" (29 months). Her division of her activities (31 months) into written language and drawing caused questions to separate into types as well. "What does this say?" and "What did you write?" could be directed at what adults could judge to be writing samples, and "Tell me about this picture," and "What did you draw?" could be applied to her drawings.

Giti's increasing interest in letter writing might be considered the development of her responsibility for the maintenance of totally written communication. However, while she could write and draw on her own, the point at which a balance in child-caregiver roles was achieved is more difficult to determine than with oral language and early reading. The need to produce and the need to conform to a mutually comprehensible graphic code continue to make the role of the model more important for written language in terms of consciously sustained effort than in oral language and reading.

Giti used oral language and writing as mutually reinforcing processes. Initially "me" or "papa" was used to get her a pen and some paper. We used oral language to identify the products to her, so she could expect written language to be as meaningful as oral language. What I said could be written down and by extension, what she thought could be written down. Through having adults write and label what they had done and by asking her what she had done, she began to realize her creations deserved names. Her earliest labels were "Snoopy" and "cat" (21 months). By 24 months, labeling her mountain peaks "McDonald's" and "Marce," she had started to use relationships between sounds and letters to write (C.

Chomsky, 1976; Gentry, 1981; Read, 1975b; Zutell, 1978). At 26 months she identified drawing with grandparents and asked them to draw, and writing with us and asked us to write. Her oral language could elicit samples of drawing and writing to teach her to separate the categories of drawing and writing and to refine them. In addition to demanding total products, she demanded dictations of lists of single words as examples from which to learn (27 months). Having heard her name spelled out and numbers uttered aloud, she would practice writing and simultaneously accompany the writing with a sing-song of letters and numbers. For more than one year she had been

Dawn
United States

Najeeba
Saudi Arabia

Reprinted with permission of Jerome C. Harste and Robert F. Carey.

Dalia
Egypt

Giti
27 months

Figure 34. Uninterrupted writing samples from young English and Arabic speakers

Baghban

sounding like an English speaking child and she was speaking English. Now (27 months) her writing began to look like English. In fact, Giti's written language compares favorably with that of Dawn's, and both samples contrast with early writing samples from preschool native speakers of Arabic (see Figure 34).

At 28 months Giti extended her interactions with oral and written language from dictations in isolation to dictations in the context of a waitress game. Playing waitress required the presence of another person and school needed stuffed animals and dolls. Even when language learners are physically alone, they can assume counterparts with which to practice dialogue (Weir, 1962).

Once Giti identified oral language and written language as partners and established the communicative nature of writing more firmly, she could move on to the totally written language interaction found in her letter writing. Her labeling of her letters expanded from one word, "Grandma" (27 months), to "This is a letter from Grandma. She be happy. You save it." (31 months). In oral language she had moved from a one word label to sentences, and she could now apply the same information to the context of written language. The early label denoted a general intent while the later label showed that she had written, specifically a letter, and directed it at a particular person, her grandmother. As an extension of how Giti felt when she got mail, she declared that her grandmother would appreciate it. I was always saving letters and Giti's writing, so she should save this product as well. Giti's oral language had helped her build a schema for written language and its functions, particularly letter writing. In turn, what Giti considered to be involved in the schema could be demonstrated in her oral language by a kind of thinking outloud. Giti used oral and written language to make her experiences amenable to conceptual treatment, and her concepts were reflected in how she handled experiences.

Giti also used reading and writing as mutually reinforcing processes. Initially she perceived our written linguistic symbols. The development of control in her scribbling from 18-20 months demonstrates that she had seen writing samples and realized she did not have to completely fill a sheet of paper with her marks. She noted circles and dots which she added to her products. With her writing on print (21 months), she discriminated writing from anything else on paper and the different contexts where writing might occur. Gradually she separated her writing from the print, but she could also practice on the same page, reading the model silently as it appeared near her product. By practicing book babbling on her own writing (24 months), she demonstrated her understanding that what she had written was meaningful and could be read. Giti not only read her writing as a total pattern aloud, but she must have read silently the *m* in Kmart, identified it orally as "onalds," and then attempted to reproduce it on paper. Enough exposure to her own name printed by adults and in her name puzzle prompted recognition and reproduction of *G* (25 months). At 26 months she could discriminate differences in length between *Giti* and *Grandma*.

In the sense that discrimination of graphic input and localization for opportunities to reproduce it may be considered facets of early writing, similar parallels can be found in drawing. Based on visual input, Giti had to decide when adults were writing and when they were drawing. Very much like children in bilingual homes who identify one language with each parent in order to develop two distinct linguistic means of communication, Giti identified drawing with her grandparents and writing with us (26 months). Once she had separated these two types of graphic input, she could concentrate on clarifying her productions of them. The receptive aspect of her language development had aided the productive needs. In turn, now what Giti created, based on two separate schemata, she could recognize.

According to Cattell's scale of infant intelligence (1960), the average child will scribble spontaneously at 18 months when given paper and pencil or earlier if also given a demonstration of how to write. Giti had adult models and demonstrations, so she could support this observation with her initial scribbling at 17 months. Her stages or levels of writing were similar to those noted by Hildreth (1936) and Legrun (1932): unorganized scribbles (Figure 1), scribbles with vertical and horizontal tendencies (Figure 3), consistent linearity (Figure 6), a variety of unbroken structures (Figure 13), and units with real or approximations to real letters (Figure 27). Lavine (1972) summarized such results by noting that many preschool children produce "forms that contain features characteristic of writing and not of pictures—linearity and horizontal orientation. Many of this age also produce variation of height" (p. 25). Giti had developed her schema for the flow of English in written language by 27 months, recognized by adults and labeled by her as "writing." She continues to refine her idea of HOW ENGLISH LOOKS WHEN WRITTEN DOWN by discovering the units within this pattern.

How did drawing manage to assert its own identity? Giti's oral language base, experience with reading, and exposure to writing and drawing models provided the raw material. By 21 months she realized that people labeled their activities with paper and implements as well as the products they produced. When questioned about what her scribbles might be, she answered "Snoopy" or "cat." At 24 months, she began to associate the sounds she could hear and produce with the letters she could read and produce (M and G). However, it was not until she successfully identified drawing with grandparents and writing with her parents (27 months) that independent understandings of the two processes could be observed. At 27 months she had captured the flow of English on paper (Figure 13). HOW ENGLISH LOOKS WHEN WRITTEN DOWN, as interpreted by Giti, would be labeled by an adult as "writing." Babbling in oral language served to produce HOW PEOPLE SOUND WHEN THEY TALK, and her book babbling led to BOOKS TALK IN A SPECIAL WAY (Chapter 3). Scribbling, which apparently led to a written language pattern in which English looks like English, can be considered their parallel. Once Giti achieved this pattern for writing, she could begin to characterize a basic pattern for drawing. Interestingly, adults observing her products from 27-31 months could label them either writing or drawing, but Giti chose not to do so. At 27 months she could differentiate the products her mother produced in the frustrating sequences when she ordered, "Write *Grandma*." but really meant, "Draw Grandma." It was not until Giti was 31 months old that she used her speech to correctly label her own activities. Table 3 summarizes the stages of her written language development.

Because it has been noted that Giti simultaneously used her linguistic processes to support and reinforce each other, it is important to contrast oral language, reading, and written language in their longitudinal development. Table 4 combines Table 1 (Chapter 3) with Table 3 (Chapter 4).

Table 3
Development of Written Language

Approximate Age in Months	Written Language
17	Paper and pen handling; unorganized scribbling (Figure 1)
20	Vertical and horizontal scribbling (Figure 3)
21	Labels "Snoopy," "cat," and "writing" indiscriminately (Figure 5)
24	Consistent linearity; sound-letter associations (Figure 8)
26	Categorization of writing and drawing with people
27	Writing schema; Giti perceives and labels her writing as writing (Figure 13)
29	Adults distinguish her products as writing or drawing (Figures 17, 18, 19)
31	Giti perceives and labels her products as writing or drawing (Figure 23)

Table 4
Chronological Comparison of Oral Language, Reading, and Written Language Development

Approximate Age in Months	Oral Language	Approximate Age in Months	Reading	Approximate Age in Months	Written Language
9	babbling	14	book babbling	17	scribbling
12	labeling in environment	14	labeling in books	21	labeling products
15	associations in environment	20	associations across books	24	associations of sounds and letters
20	categorizations in environment	25	categorizations of printed items	26	categorization of writing and drawing
30	storytelling schema	30	story reading schema	27	writing schema
				31	drawing schema

Baghban

Table 4 shows that each of Giti's communicative processes began with attempts at reproducing linguistic models which later resulted in a basic schema for processing appropriate lingustic input. Initially she tested hypotheses by labeling, then associating and categorizing the raw data she experienced in her environment. Evidently once she could categorize the activity and locate it in her cognitive structure, the separation of the schema could proceed. Giti experienced periods of confusion and frustration just before this separation occurred. At the beginning of her 27th month after her grandparents had left, her commands for writing and drawing conflicted with whatever she wanted me to produce. By the end of the same month, this frustration disappeared and she could use the label "writing" for her written language products consistently. At 30 months, she suddenly seemed to be drawing her letters to people and she would use oral language such as "Here's a wall and a pond. Flowers." for indications of drawing (Figure 21). She would not label these activities "drawing." In her 31st month she used, "I drawing" for her activities which she felt were drawing and her letter writing returned to linear expansions. The two periods of confusion (27 months and 30 months) just before her clarification of her understandings of "writing" and "drawing" respectively parallel the period in her oral language development from 28-29 months when it was difficult to understand her speech just before the clarification of her understandings of "storytelling" and "storyreading." Apparently whatever process existed got temporarily clouded by the schemata about to emerge. Interestingly, by 34 months her writing went from left to right again, but kept the top to bottom orientation. Once she correctly and consistently categorized drawing (31 months), she could continue to refine her writing schemata to approximate the models around her. Because these understandings seemed to be separating themselves during the same period (28-31 months), it is no wonder that Giti experienced difficulty communicating orally.

Because Giti's early graphic activities have been considered to be writing, we may ask, "Just when did she begin to write?" Once she made a connection between the movements of the pen and the traces on paper, and she was assured that these effects could be repeated, she fell in love with their production. Once she understood that these traces could somehow be meaningful and she enjoyed producing them, she was determined to learn to write. From this point on her activities can be termed "writing," for the intent to write signaled the onset of writing in her life.

Learning to write is truly an act of self-discovery. Oral language is personal but strongly influenced by the immediate context which is not always determined by the individual. Thoughts and feelings are expressed in written language and also in drawings. Eng (1931, 1957) agrees that early drawing is ideomotive and children produce more realistic drawings only as their concepts become clearer and their skill increases. Buhler (1930) emphasizes verbal rather than visual presentations of reality in children's drawings and applies the word "schema" to their stylizations. Thus, Giti's drawing and writing understandings are related to each other and to the development of her thought processes and her verbal abilities as manifested in her oral language. The interconnection of the language arts rests indisputable.

When was the onset of readiness to write? Giti had to be physically capable of holding a pen in one hand and positioning a piece of paper with the other. Small fingers had greater ease holding small implements. In this physiological sense, readiness to write is similar to readiness to talk since both processes are dependent on the maturation of specific organs and muscles. In reading, someone can hold a book for you, and provided you can see or touch, you can be exposed to print. In speaking and writing, you must perform yourself. When the physiological development is achieved, readiness, even as a state of being rather than a time period, remains difficult to define. As with all learning, motivation and exposure appear to be the indelible factors that determine readiness to write. Typical labels are inadequate.

In summary, the speech act dialogue orientation, with interactions manipulated by the caregivers, fits the early action-dialogue contexts of written language as well as oral language and reading. Table 5 indicates that as an outgrowth of dialogue, the child continues to test hypotheses in order to refine schema which in turn continue to influence her information-processing strategies and her oral language interactions.

Table 5

Model of the Development of Written Language and Drawing Schemata

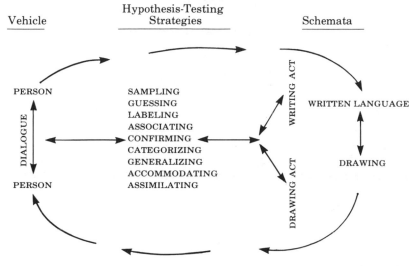

Table 5 summarizes Giti's written language development in the first three years of her life. Her success with dialogue as a vehicle for handling her early environment led naturally to the use of interaction as an approach to early writing. Realizing the value of her play with paper and pen for communication, she applied her oral language learning strategies, which she was also using in learning to read, to written language situations. As her physiological and cognitive development advanced, and her strategies became more complex, she subdivided her broad linguistic framework in written language into two schemata useful to her life: one for written language contexts and one for drawing.

Giti continues to acquire language in order to understand the normative character of her shared world (Cook-Gumperz, 1975). As a participating member in a literate society, she had separated, before her third birthday, the contexts of oral language and reading (Chapter 3) and written language and

Table 6

Summary of Storytelling, Story Reading, Written Language, and Drawing Development

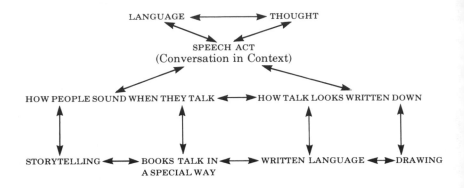

drawing (Chapter 4) within her total communicative model. Table 6 summarizes the developmental relations of Giti's oral language, reading, writing, and drawing.

Based on the need to survive, Giti developed oral language through interaction with her environment. Conversations in context provided her with opportunities to try out strategies which helped more efficiently process her experiences. Convinced that the speech act was a meaningful experience and that oral language was an active, creative, personal form of expression, she continued to learn from communicative situations. From her aural perceptions, she conceived the idea of HOW PEOPLE SOUND WHEN THEY TALK, and from her visual perceptions, she conceived the idea of HOW TALK LOOKS WRITTEN DOWN. She used these schemata as support systems. Having books read to her and stories told to her, Giti further refined her idea of HOW PEOPLE SOUND WHEN THEY TALK into how people sound when they read books aloud or BOOKS TALK IN A SPECIAL WAY, and how people sound when they tell a story or STORYTELLING. Having people write words for her and send her letters, Giti further refined her idea of HOW TALK LOOKS WRITTEN DOWN into a category for composing WRITTEN LANGUAGE. Drawing has a verbal, ideographic core for a young child. With continuous experience in having people draw for her, Giti supports this conclusion by refining her notion of HOW TALK LOOKS WRITTEN DOWN into a category for DRAWING. These discourse contexts can only continue to support each other and her communicative model as a whole as Giti grows.

Perspective

Early Reading and Writing Are Social

Giti's early social interactions gave her the raw material to use in her discovery of the world. From context-bound messages in which verbal and nonverbal elements contributed to meaning, she used semantic intent to build her vocabulary within developing syntactic rules. As parents, we emphasized meaning in our communications to her and in our expectations from her. Through her interactions with us, she learned that her oral language had to have a semantic core to be of communicative value. She learned to understand as well as to expect understanding from other people.

Giti kept her early reading as social and functional as her speaking. She sat on our laps or next to us while we read to her and talked about the stories and pictures. The success of our reading to her surely derived from the extra opportunity the experience provided for body contact along with the conversation. The pleasure she found in the coziness of our reading to her has transferred to the comfort she herself now finds in the act of reading. Moreover, she has always made us aware that she considered dialogue a necessary characteristic for reading. When she was a toddler, if we were reading newspapers or magazines, she took the event as an act of withdrawal and slapped down our reading material. At five years, she still felt we were ignoring her if we read silently. She, on the other hand, always read *to* us while traveling in the car. If alone in her room, she read *to* her parakeets or her dolls.

Giti kept her writing as social and functional as her speaking and reading. She wrote sitting beside us or lying on the floor near us. After she wrote a single letter or a word, she showed it to us saying, "See" or "Look" and invited us to view her writing and respond to it. She asked us to write the words she was interested in seeing in print, and her two most common questions about writing were, "How do you spell _____?" and "Is this how you spell _____?" The interaction she understood in the nature of the writing context, she expanded to the dialogue in her waitress game and letter writing.

Language Learning Is Easier with a Proficient Model

Giti was able to have one-to-one relationships with us, her parents, as adult users of language who value reading and writing. It is a truism that anyone learns anything, whether reading or tennis, easier in frequent interaction with a model who is more proficient than the learner. For instance, Giti's writing immediately after seeing her father write (Figure 4) and her drawing snowfigures immediately after seeing her grandmother draw (Figure 23) indicate more proficiency than she demonstrated on her own in writing or drawing at those times. If Giti had been one of many children, opportunities for the sustained dialogue which was her principal vehicle of learning would have been reduced. Because we care about her, we are interested in fostering her mastery of language so that we can better communicate and learn to know each other. By listening to her, answering her questions, reading to her, writing notes to her, providing books and writing materials for her, and locating opportunities for library storyhours and membership in book clubs, we create an environment that encourages enthusiasm for the language arts.

Stories Aid Comprehension

A universal function of language is the telling of stories. A sense of story is crucial to human development because

> We resort to story to make an entity of experience; to give our experience form and balance; to make generalizations about the world. We structure and often modify experience when creating stories of our everyday life, and also, often modify our own internal representations of experience when listening to the stories of others. (Brown, 1975, p. 357)

Giti grew up listening to stories as part of our family life. Questions such as "How was your day?" and "What happened then?" triggered personal experience stories. We made up stories such as "When your birthday comes..." and retold the stories of her books. The majority of her books were storybooks (see the Bibliography of Giti's Books). By 30 months, Giti told stories and her oral reading demonstrated a real search for plot in the text. She could bring her life experiences and her oral language experiences to the storybooks. The storybooks reinforced her knowledge of the world through their predictability, which in turn aided her ability to make appropriate syntactic and semantic guesses when reading. The storybooks also expanded her knowledge of the world through indirect experiences, so that even at a very young age she was able to learn through written language. By four years of age, she applied her sense of story to drawing and writing contexts. Even at 5 years of age she told stories about her pictures and wrote her own stories in books she made herself. As a cognitive organizer, a sense of story certainly has implications for the learning of the language arts. Experience with stories aids the predictability necessary for successful reading and listening, and a model of the elements in a story aids the composing inherent in writing and speaking.

The Language Arts Are Interdependent Support Systems

The intuitive use by children of all available data to maintain the communicative intent of messages has been termed "negotiability" (Harste, et al., 1979b). According to this concept, what is known about one communication system supports growth in other communication systems. Giti certainly demonstrated this ability in her language development.

At first, oral language satisfied her immediate needs, but once she recognized the value of reading and writing for communication, the processes became intersupportive. Giti used the relationships between the processes to define and categorize contexts for speaking, reading, writing, and drawing acts. Once she localized the contexts, she could keep defining each system. Apparently in order to get it all together, she had to first figure out each category. Therefore, her reading and writing did not appear as second order abstractions of oral language. They were independent schemata triggered directly by thought and bound by their respective discourse contexts within her communicative model.

Giti used oral language, reading, writing, and drawing as partners within a larger system of mutually reinforcing processes. Her experience with the rhymes and songs she had learned orally helped her locate them in her books. As her experiences broadened, she used the books to help her categorize and label items and events in her enviroment. Her application of "motor boats" and "sail boats" seen in books to real boats on a lake demonstrated that the limited experience of a very young child can be expanded through print. Similarly, oral language supported Giti's early writing. She said, "Me," or /papa/ to get the paper and a pen to write, and then sang as she scribbled. Later she demanded dictations and initiated her waitress-game as a situation in which talking and writing were complementary. By practicing book-babbling on her own writing, Giti demonstrated her understanding that what she had written was meaningful and could be read, and she had to have been able to reading M and G in order to practice writing them as her favorite letters. Her writing and drawing were reproductions of letters, objects, and people she perceived, and she used her oral language to label them. Through all her activities, she showed that she was simultaneously involved in the learning of oral language, reading, and writing (Table 4).

The Language Learner Directs Her Own Learning

Holdaway (1979, p. 14) describes active learning.

> Developmental learning which is highly individual and noncompetitive, short on teaching and long on learning, self-regulated rather than adult-regulated, goes hand-in-hand with the fulfillment of real life purposes, and emulates the behavior of people who model the skill in natural use.

We learn best what we discover ourselves, and language learners personalize models of comprehension. Our own interest instigates and maintains activity and, provided what we learn finds a function in our lives, we continue to direct our own learning.

Giti selected books to read, questioned plots in the books, demanded dictations, initiated the waitress-game, wrote letters to us, and set up school. She determined the occasion for these activities and the amount of time she spent on them. She asked questions, she made decisions, and she persisted in her language learning. Whenever she wanted, she could have given up reading and writing as uninteresting. Particularly at 27 months before her clarification of storytelling and reading, and at 30 months before her clarification of writing and drawing, her frustration was so intense that it might have been easier for her to give up. Yet her need to communicate through reading and writing demonstrated the value she placed on these processes, and her frustration instead stimulated cognitive clarification. We waited and she worked out her schemata.

Language Learners Need to Know That They Know

Giti is linguistically aware. She has grasped the inter-relations of the language arts and she knows when and where each of her schema may function. If refused the reading of a coloring book because there is no story in it, she defends her choice with, "But there are words." How could a book with words NOT be read? At the library she selects her books with the criterion, "They have not too many words," and her writing demonstrates that "Giti" is a shorter word than "Grandma." Not only does she have a concept of the absence or presence of print, quantity of print, and word length, but she can apply social judgments to expressions as well. She rates, "dumb," "stupid," and "goofball" as "bad words" because she has been told they are bad words. She will be sad if anyone applies these words to her and can tease us by applying such words to us. When listening, she has a notion of correctness or match. Her productions, "/memiy/ do it" (for "Let me do it"), and "I lub you" (for "I love you"), or "I want to go to the wobby" (for "I want to go to the lobby") are unquestioned as she utters them. If either of us teases her by repeating the sentences her way, Giti applies a mental touchstone, she scolds us, "No, no, no," and attempts to correct us. Thus, she demonstrates metalinguistic knowledge on semantic, syntactic, and graphophonemic levels which are constantly developing, and we add to our surprise and her happiness by commenting to her on how much she knows about language and how language works.

In fact, we can honestly emphasize how much she knows because we focus on the function or message of what she says or writes. By recognizing that at her age she cannot possibly have control of correct form, we encourage her understanding of communication. The axiom, "Nothing succeeds like success," is a good rule for learning. Giti feels she can handle oral and written language and her attitude can only motivate her learning. She reads and writes on her own. When she gets up in the morning, she reads outloud to her dolls. She leaves us notes in the hall closet. Her competence is ever-expanding.

Drawing Is the Fifth Language Art

There is some evidence that stability encourages exploratory behavior, a good self-image, a perception of effective adults, and a grasp of logic and order in the world (Gibson & Levin, 1975, pp. 268-269). Giti's home environment followed by a fixed weekday routine. She knew the overall pattern of her days, could predict what was going to happen, and would question, "Where we going?" or "Why?" for any deviations. Giti was able to take advantage of the everyday stability in her environment to experiment in art. Ideally, drawing provides a context which is exploratory for young children, while traditionally reading and writing contexts are more restricted. However, the flexibility Giti enjoyed in her early reading and writing was no less limited than in her drawing. This freedom allowed to her to direct her own learning and to understand the functions of each context by making connections herself.

For Giti, drawing is a separate communicative context. Her drawing like writing, began with motor control of an instrument capable of producing marks on paper. She used her experiences to create a whole product. For the young artist, the person or object to be drawn must be nearby and visible in order to produce a representation. For the young writer, examples of letters must be immediately available to replicate print. As the artist-writer matures, production moves toward decontextualization and the symbol systems and their use become internalized.

Both drawing and writing use graphic codes through which other people can understand the producer's inspiration. The distinction between the processes is crucial. For example, a wavy line may look at one point like a series of the letter "m," but if extended, the line becomes ocean waves. Moreover, drawn and written products are read. The perceiver samples in order to construct the meanings and feelings the artist or writer wishes to communicate. The mature reader, like the mature artist or writer, moves toward decontextualization, but, in this instance, to reconstruct the intention of what is already created rather than to create.

Child's Play Is Purposeful

The influence of play in child development is enormous. Montessori said, "Play is child's work." By this she meant

> physical and mental activity freely chosen by an individual— activity that has meaning for [her] because it promotes [her] own growth or contributes to society. (Lillard, 1972, p. 139)

Play appeals to the child's orientation to action when language is little developed, channels currents of physical energy into productive forces, and provides a freedom and spontaneity not often found in daily life.

Giti began to use oral language because of need, but reading and writing began as play activities. Her play was rarely without meaning and catered in actuality to her persistent curiosity and changing interests. It gave a focus to dialogue. Once she realized through interaction that reading and writing could satisfy communicative needs, she determined to learn them. When she understood that oral language such as rhymes could be entertaining, she practiced reciting them. When she realized getting mail was fun, she corresponded. Giti never separated function from fun in her learning of the language arts. The more she read and wrote, the more pleasure she derived from reading and writing. In this way, the cognitive aspects of play and the pleasurable aspects of reading and writing reinforce each other, and learning through play fosters the joy inherent in learning to read and write.

Reading Requires a Developmental Definition

The lap method (Moffett & Wagner, 1976) in which a parent, grandparent, or sibling holds a small child and reads aloud to her takes place in many families. Giti, accustomed to this practice as a toddler, chose a book, stood in front of someone she decided could read, and backed up to the reader. Parents I have met casually since this case study have frequently commented that their toddlers did the same to initiate reading.

At eighteen months, Giti would pick up a book from the floor, put it rightside up, and turn pages from left to right. Such early book handling in other children has been documented on videotape (Hill, 1979). This kind of top-bottom, left-right orientation would not have occurred if Giti had been in a language group which did not represent its print with such directionality.

When did Giti begin to read? Smith (1971) declares that reading begins with the first word the child can recognize. According to Ryan (1977, p. 159), "When a child responds to a common symbol around the house, beginning reading should be considered to be occurring." We need only to recall Helen Keller's connecting the water pump on her hand to the word "water" to agree with Emery (1975, p. 113) that "The step from understanding no language symbol to knowing just a few is a large one." The matching of a word heard in the passage of time to a word seen localized in space is a monumental task. And yet, until a child conforms to an adult definition of reading, most people will not call that child a reader. Interestingly, a child will utter a single word, and proud relatives declare her "talking." If many two-year-olds (Baghban, 1979; Divita, 1980; Gibson & Levin, 1975; Ryan, 1977) recognize the signs for fast food restaurants, cereals, stores, etc., then this is reading for two-year-olds exposed to a rich print environment. *Zoo, stop, Kroger, Sears, milk, thank you, in, out, Boys, Girls, Ladies, Men, Enter, Exit* appear to be common sight words for preschoolers (Cooper, 1981; Divita, 1980). In addition to her broader environment, Giti used the same dictionary books and labels in the pictures of other books with which she had built up her oral vocabulary to increase her sight vocabulary in reading.

By three years of age, Giti could look at the pictures of a favorite book and produce the story, retaining the original meaning of the text and including dialogue. She read to us and to dolls in storytime fashion, beginning with "Once upon a time" or "One day" and was careful to add "The End" at the end. Parent-researchers have documented such story schema demonstrations with other three-year-olds (Cooper, 1981; Cohn, 1981; Divita, 1980).

This case study ended at 34 months. However, during Giti's fourth year, she seemed compelled to say something as she turned each page of a book. At that time she had favorite books that she wanted to listen to over and over, even at the same sitting. She also would supply the words in the stories if overlooked. She could recognize familar sight words in various print and sizes. Parents and parent-researchers of other four-year-olds have often observed such behaviors (Cooper, 1981; Divita, 1980). By 4.9 years, Giti "took off" reading Bright and Early Books with smooth intonation and speed. At 5 years she could handle Amelia Bedelia, Little Monster, folktales and some of *Newsweek*. She questioned vocabulary such as "looked puzzled," "cackled," or "It's none of your business," but gave the impression of being able to tackle just about any kind of print.

Giti's reading began with gross approximations to print and became successively refined until she more closely matched adult definitions of reading through her ease in handling written materials. But at each stage, Giti intended to read when she engaged in reading activities and she thought of herself as reading. The other children documented at 18 months and 2, 3, and 4 years also considered themselves to be reading. Because researchers agree that reading follows stages, and children at approximately the same age behave with print in a similar fashion across their age group (Clay, 1975; Holdaway, 1979), adults should also call them readers. Terms such as "prereading," "emergent reading," "reading-like," "learning to read," "imitative reading," and "reading" in quotation marks should be dismissed from the literature on natural readers. They *are* reading.

Writing Requires a Developmental Definition

Giti began to scribble at 17 months. According to Cattell's (1960) scale of infant intelligence, the average child will scribble spontaneously at 18 months when given paper and pencil or earlier if given a demonstration of how to write. Because Giti had adult models and writing demonstrations, the physical ability to hold a writing instrument, and the materials available, she could support this observation. She began with unorganized scribbles and moved to scribbles with vertical and horizontal tendencies. Such a transition has been documented for early writers (Clay, 1975; Hildreth, 1936; Legrun, 1932), and many parents note a love of playing with circles at this time (Goffin, 1981). By the end of her second year, Giti demonstrated consistent linearity in her writing. She asked for the names of letters she saw. This activity proceeded toward a variety of unbroken structures to units with real or approximations to real letters during her third year (Clay, 1975; Cooper, 1981; Divita, 1980; Hildreth, 1936; Legrun, 1932).

Parent-researchers have documented support activities such as playing teacher or waitress, writing letters and typing strings of letters (Cooper, 1981; Divita, 1980; Goffin, 1981; Hutchinson, 1981). Typical of early writers, Giti wrote her own name first. By four years of age, her favorite vocabulary for notes was "Hi," "me," "Baba," "Mommy," "I love you." At the same time, she filled piles of paper practicing with letters of the alphabet with various orientations, in lists and from left to right or right to left. She could write anything if spelled for her. She used the same dictionary books with which she had first learned oral labels and gained a sight vocabulary, as sources from which to copy other needed words. By 5 years she began to guess at the spellings of words using consonants. Interestingly, when her activity in writing peaked, her activity in reading temporarily lessened and vice versa. Other parent-researchers have also noted that their children seem able to maintain heightened activity in only one process at a time and take turns engaging more often in reading or in writing (Cooper, 1981; Divita, 1980).

When did Giti begin to write? Once she could hold a writing instrument, with each activity she intended to write and considered herself to be writing. The other children documented at 18 months, 2, 3, and 4 years also considered themselves to be writing. Because researchers agree that writing follows stages and children at approximately the same age behave with print in a similar fashion across their age group (Clay, 1975; Gentry, 1981), adults should also call them writers. Terms such as "prewriting," "mock writing," "writing like," "learning to write," and "writing" in quotation marks should be dismissed from the literature on natural writers. They *are* writing.

"Readiness" Is an Inappropriate Term in Developmental Literacy

Giti read because print existed in her environment and she was introduced to pleasurable reading activities. Given her natural curiosity, exposure to people who wrote in front of her, and the physical capacity to hold a writing implement, she began to write. While the definitions of reading and writing literally run the gamut, in Giti's case the intent to read and the intent to write are common starting points. Durkin (1963) recommends that the best way to assess a child's readiness for learning to read is to give the child the opportunity to do so. Gibson and Levin (1975) concur that given children's natural curiosity, they should be considered ready to extract information from the printed page as soon as they have the opportunity to look at any book and hear someone read. It follows then that seeing someone write, and having materials available with the physical ability to use them, determines readiness to write. In this sense, the only criteria which might then be considered readiness-related are the child's interest and the availability of reading and writing models and materials. No other preparation is necessary for an encounter with print.

Insight into the Encounter with Print

The encouragement of a proficient reader and writer may lead children to literacy early. The home can foster reading and writing as positive, natural, exciting play shared by children and their families. Yet the same family may produce both early readers and nonreaders. Moreover, early readers and writers may be found in environments which do not facilitate interest in print. Elusive factors within children appear to be important to the development of literacy (Teale, 1978).

Children who read early have been rated by parents as 1) persistent, 2) perfectionistic, 3) eager to keep up, 4) high strung, and 5) curious (Durkin, 1973). While the IQs of natural readers are not necessarily higher than average, children's persistence, their auditory and visual memories, their language development, and their interest may provide the confidence to proceed and the assurance that print is something they can work out for themselves. Research on cognition (Briggs & Elkind, 1973; Polk & Goldstein, 1980) indicates that early readers may be in the stage of concrete operations. If accurate, such cognitive differences may influence the processing of print.

Parents' observations (Clark, 1976) that the early reader does not make out the sounds of letters and work out words "pronouncing like a child," but rather "it just click(s)," holds true for Giti and for several of her friends. In fact, the most commonly shared expression of the parents is that their children just "took off" reading. The difference in processing ability for these children is apparently heavily dependent on a large sight vocabulary which happens to match the print materials they encounter. Giti loves to read familiar stories so that she may say, "I can read as fast as you." Smith (1971) and Kavale and Screiner (1978) discuss the desirability of compiling a large stock of sight words so that initial reading is more fluid. Both sources also emphasize that overloading the short term memory with attention to detail can result in an overall loss of comprehension and information. Indeed, my own experience with Giti's reading at 5 years of age verifies this assumption with her own words. When she comes to an unknown word in a new book and is encouraged to sound it out, she exclaims "You're making me forget the story. Just tell me, I'll remember it next time." Speed and fluency therefore enhance the pleasure inherent in the process, and keep the act of reading self-reinforcing.

The wealth of specific data collected over the first 34 months of Giti's life suggests that continued research by trained parents using a case study approach offers as much to language arts education as it does to child language research, as both fields struggle to construct accurate models of children's oral and written language development. In the search to describe the processes, we must remind ourselves never to underestimate children as learners. If very young learners can informally direct their own progress and use what they *have* learned to gain control of what they *are* learning, the least each of us can do is to keep alive in classrooms the

meaning inherent in oral and written language interaction—
and the pleasure that comes from the understanding of such
interactions.

Bibliography

Aaronson, D., & Reiber, R.W. (Eds.). *Developmental psycholinguistics and communication disorders.* Annals of New York Academy of Science, 1975, 263.

Abravanel, Eugene. Action imitation: The early phase of infancy. *Child Development,* 1976, *47,* 1032-1044.

Adams, Marilyn Jager, & Collins, Allan. *A schema theoretic view of reading* (Tech. Rep. #32). Urbana: Center for the Study of Reading, University of Illinois at Urbana-Champaign, April 1977.

Ainsworth, M.D.S., & Bell, S.M. Mother-infant interaction and the development of competence. In K. Connolly & J. Bruner (Eds.), *The growth of competence.* New York: Academic Press, 1974, 97-119.

Albright, R.W., & Albright, J.B. Application of descriptive linguistics to child language. *Journal of Speech and Hearing Research,* 1958, *1,* 257-261.

Albright, R.W., & Albright, J.B. The phonology of a two-year-old child. *Word,* 1956, *12,* 382-390.

Allen, R.R., & Brown, Kenneth L. *Developing communicative competence in children.* Skokie, Illinois: National Textbook Company, 1976.

Alloway, T., Krames, L., & Pliner, P. *Communication and affect: A comparative approach.* New York: Academic Press, 1972.

Almy, M., Chittenden, E., & Miller, P. *Young children's thinking.* New York: Teachers College Press, 1967.

Almy, Millie C. *Children's experiences prior to first grade and success in beginning reading.* New York: Teachers College Press, 1949.

Almy, Millie C. Children's experiences prior to first grade and success in beginning reading. *Teachers College Record,* 1950, *51,* 392-393.

Almy, Millie C. *Ways of studying children.* New York: Columbia Teachers College Press, 1959.

Ames, Louise B. Free drawing and completion drawing: A comparative study of preschool children. *Journal of Genetic Psychology,* 1945, *66,* 161-165.

Amidon, E.J., & Hough, J.B. (Eds.). *Interaction analysis: Theory, research and application.* Reading, Masschusetts: Addison-Wesley, 1967.

Anastasiow, Nicholas J. Cognition and language: Some observations. In James C. Laffey and Roger Shuy (Eds.), *Language differences: Do they interfere?* Newark, Delaware: International Reading Association, 1973, 17-25.

Anastasiow, Nicholas J. *Oral language: Expression of thought.* Newark, Delaware: International Reading Association, 1971.

Anderson, Richard C., Reynolds, Ralph E., Schallert, Diane L. & Goetz, Ernest T. Frameworks for comprehending discourse. *American Educational Research Journal,* 1977, *14,* 367-381.

Andrews, Nancy. *Six case studies in learning to read.* Unpublished doctoral dissertation, Indiana University, 1976.

Anglin, Jeremy M. *The growth of word meaning.* Cambridge, Massachusetts: MIT, Press, 1970.

Anglin, Jeremy M. *Word, object, and conceptual development.* New York: Norton, 1977.

Antinucci, Francesco, & Parisi, Domenico. Early language acquisition: A model and some data. In Charles A. Ferguson & Dan I. Slobin (Eds.), *Studies of child language development.* New York: Holt, Rinehart and Winston, 1973, 607-627.

Antinucci, Francesco, & Parisi, Domenico. Early semantic development in child language. In Eric H. Lenneberg & Elizabeth Lenneberg (Eds.), *Foundations of language development: A multidisciplinary approach 1.* New York: Academic Press, 1975, 189-201.

Appplebee, Arthur N. *The child's concept of story.* Chicago: University of Chicago Press, 1978.

Artley, A. Sterl. Oral language growth and reading ability. *Elementary School Journal,* 1953, *53,* 321-328.

Ashton-Warner, Sylvia. *Teacher.* New York: Simon and Schuster, 1963.

Athey, Irene J. Language models and reading. *Reading Research Quarterly,* 1971, *7,* 16-110.

Athey, Irene J. Reading reseach in the affective domain. In Harry Singer & Robert Ruddell (Eds.), *Theoretical Models and Processes of Reading.* Newark, Delaware: International Reading Association, 1976, 352-380.

Athey, Irene J. Synthesis of papers on language development and reading. *Reading Research Quarterly,* 1971, *7,* 9-15.

Athey, Irene J. Theories of language development and their relation to reading. In Frank P. Greene (Ed.), *Reading: The Right to Participate.* Milwaukee, Wisconsin: National Reading Conference, 1971.

Auckerman, Robert C. (Ed.). *Some persistent questions on beginning reading.* Newark, Delaware: International Reading Association, 1972.

Austerlitz, R. Gilyak. Nursery words. *Word,* 1965, *12,* 260-279.

Austin, J.L. *How to do things with words.* New York: Oxford University Press, 1962.

Baghban, Marcia. *Language development and initial encounters with written language: A case study in preschool reading and writing.* Dissertation, Indiana University, 1979.

Bar-Adon, Aaron, & Leopold, Werner F. (Eds.). *Child language: A book of readings.* Englewood Cliffs, New Jersey: Prentice-Hall, 1971.

Bar-Hillel, Yehoshua (Ed.). *Pragmatics of natural languages.* Dordrecht, Holland: D. Reidel Publishing, 1971.

Barker, R. (Ed.). *Stream of behavior.* New York: Appleton-Century-Crofts, 1963.

Barr, A.S. The case study method in education. *Journal of Educational Research,* 1930, *22,* 59-60.

Barr, Rebecca. Processes underlying the learning of printed words. *Elementary School Journal,* 1975, *75,* 258-268.

Bates, Elizabeth. *Language and context: The acquisition of pragmatics.* New York: Academic Press, 1976a.

Bates, Elizabeth. Pragmatics and sociolinguistics in child language. In Donald Morehead & Ann Morehead (Eds.), *Deficient child language.* Baltimore: University Park Press, 1976b.

Bateson, M.C. Mother infant exchanges: The epigenesis of conversational interaction. In D. Aaronson & R.W. Rieber (Eds.), *Developmental Psycholinguistics and communication disorders. Annals of New York Academy of Science,* 1975, *263,* 101-113.

Beers, J., & Beers, C. Vowel spelling strategies among first and second graders: A growing awareness of written words. *Language Arts,* 1980, *57,* 166-171.

Beers, J., & Henderson, E. A study of developing orthographic concepts among first graders. *Research in the Teaching of English,* 1977, *11,* 133-148.

Beilin, Harry. *Studies in the cognitive basis of language development.* New York: Academic Press, 1975.

Bell, Silvia M. The development of the concept of object as related to infant-mother attachment. *Child Development,* 1970, *41,* 291-311.

Beller, E. Kuno. The concept readiness and several applications. *Reading Teacher,* 1970, *23,* 727-737, 747.

Bellugi, U., Klima, E.S., & Siple, P. Remembering in signs. *Cognition,* 1975, *3,* 93-125.

Bellugi, Ursula. Learning the language. *Psychology Today,* 1970, *4,* 32-35, 66.

Bennis, Warren G. The case study. *Journal of Applied Behavioral Science,* 1968, *4,* 227-231.

Berko, Jean. The child's learning of English morphology. *Word,* 1958, *14,* 150-177.

Berko, Jean, & Brown, Roger. Psycholinguistic research methods. In P.H. Mussen (Ed.), *Handbook for research methods in child development.* New York: John Wiley and Sons, 1960, 517-557.

Berlyne, D.E. A theory of human curiosity. *British Journal of Psychology,* 1954, *45,* 180-191.

Bernstein, Basil. Elaborated and restricted codes: Their social origins and some consequences. *American Anthropologist,* 1964, *66,* 55-69.

Bever, T.G. Psychologically real grammar emerges because of its role in language acquisition. In Daniel P. Dato (Ed.), *Developmental Psycholinguistics: Theory and application.* Washington, D.C.: Georgetown University, 1975, 63-75.

Biemiller, A.J. The development and use of graphic and contextual information as children learn to read. *Reading Research Quarterly,* 1970, *6,* 75-96.

Birdwhistell, R.L. *Kinesics in context.* Philadelphia: University of Pennsylvania Press, 1970.

Bishop, Jay K. The vanishing quality of the young child's learning environment. In Malcolm P. Douglass (Ed.), *Reading, thought, and language.* Claremont, California: Claremont College, 1974, 130-140.

Bissex, Glenda L. *Gnys at wrk: A child learns to write and read.* Cambridge: Harvard University Press, 1980.

Blank, M. Mastering the intangible through language. In D. Aaronson & R.W. Rieber (Eds.), *Psycholinguistics and communication disorders Annals of New York Academy of Science,* 1975, *263,* 44-58.

Block, Ruth. Aunterly love. *New York Times Magazine,* October 1, 1972.

Bloom, Lois. *Language development: Form and function in emerging grammars.* Cambridge, Massachusetts: MIT Press, 1970.

Bloom, Lois. *One word at a time.* The Hague: Mouton, 1973.

Bloom, Lois. Talking, understanding, and thinking. In Richard L. Scheifelbusch & Lyle L. Lloyd (Eds.), *Language perspectives—acquisition, retardation, and intervention.* Baltimore: University Park Press, 1974.

Bloom, Lois (Ed.). *Readings in language development.* New York: John Wiley and Sons, 1978.

Bloom, Lois, Lightbrown, Patsy, & Hood, Lois. *Structure and variation in child language.* Monograph of the *Society for Research in Child Development* #160, 1975, *40.*

Bloomfield, Leonard. *Language.* New York: Holt, Rinehart and Winston, 1933.

Blount, Ben G. Parental speech and language acquisition: Some Luo and Samoan examples. *Anthropological Linguistics,* 1972, *14,* 119-130.

Blount, Ben G. Studies in child language: An anthropological view. *American Anthropologist,* 1975, *77,* 580-600.

Bochner, A.P., & Kelley, C.W. Interpersonal competence: Rationale, philosophy and implementation of a conceptual framework. *Speech Teacher,* 1974, *23,* 279-301.

Boney, C. DeWitt. Teaching children to read as they learned to talk. *Elementary English Review,* 1939, *16,* 139-141, 156.

Bowerman, Melissa F. Development of concepts underlying language. In Richard L. Scheifelbusch & Lyle L. Lloyd (Eds.), *Language perspectives-acquisition, retardation, and intervention.* Baltimore: University Park Press, 1974, 191-209.

Bowerman, Melissa F. Semantic factors in the acquisition of rules for word use and sentence construction. In Donald M. Morehead & Ann Morehead (Eds.), Normal and deficient child language. Baltimore: University Park Press, 1976, 99-179.

Bowerman, Melissa F. Structural relationships in children's utterances: Syntactic or semantic. In Timothy E. Moore (Ed.), *Cognitive development and language acquisition.* New York: Academic Press, 1973, 197-213.

Bowers, P., & London, P. Developmental correlates of role-playing ability. *Child Development,* 1965, *36,* 499-508.

Braine, Martin D.S. *Children's first word combinations.* Chicago: University of Chicago Press, 1976.

Braine, Martin D.S. On learning the grammatical order of words. *Psychological Review,* 1963a, *70,* 323-348.

Braine, Martin D.S. The ontogeny of English phrase structure: The first phase. *Language,* 1963b, *39,* 1-13.

Brandenburg, George C. The language of a three year old child. *Pedagogical Seminary,* 1915, *22,* 89-120.

Briggs, C., & Elkind, D. Cognitive development in early readers. *Developmental Psychology,* 1973, *9,* 279-280.

Broen, Patricia Ann. *The verbal environment of the language-learning child.* Washington, D.C.: American Speech and Hearing Association, 1972.

Brown, Eric. The bases of reading acquisition. *Reading Research Quarterly,* 1970, *6,* 49-74.

Brown, Garth H. Development of story in children's reading and writing. *Theory into Practice,* 1977, *16,* 357-361.

Brown, Roger. The development of wh-questions in child speech. *Journal of Verbal Learning and Verbal Behavior,* 1968, *7,* 279-290.

Brown, Roger. *A first language: The early stages.* Cambridge, Massachusetts: Harvard University Press, 1973.

Brown, Roger. *Psycholinguistics.* New York: Free Press, 1970.

Brown, Roger. *Words and things.* Glencoe, Illinois: Free Press, 1958.

Brown, Roger, & Bellugi, Ursula. Three processes in the child's acquisition of syntax. *Harvard Educational Review,* 1964, *34,* 131-151.

Bruneau, T.J. Communicative silences: Forms and functions. *Journal of Communication,* 1973, *23,* 17-46.

Bruner, Jerome S. *Beyond the information given.* New York: W.W. Norton, 1973a.

Bruner, Jerome S. The course of cognitive growth. *American Psychologist,* 1964, *19,* 1-15.

Bruner, Jerome S. *Entry into early language: A spiral curriculum.* The Charles Gittins Memorial Lecture delivered at the University College of Swansea, 1975a.

Bruner, Jerome S. From communication to language: A psychological perspective. *Cogniton,* 1975b, *3,* 255-287.

Bruner, Jerome S. Infant education as viewed by a psychologist. In Victor H. Denenberg (Ed.), *Education of the infant and young child.* Academic Press, 1970, 109-116.

Bruner, Jerome S. Interpreting baby talk. *Time,* August 23, 1976.

Bruner, Jerome S. Learning the mother tongue. *Human Nature,* September 1978, 42-49.

Bruner, Jerome S. The ontogenesis of speech acts. *Journal of Child Language,* 1975c, *2,* 1-19.

Bruner, Jerome S. Organization of early skilled action. *Child Development,* 1973b, *44,* 1-11.

Bruner, Jerome S. *Toward a theory of instruction.* Cambridge, Massachusetts: Harvard University Press, 1966.

Bruner, Jerome S., Goodnow, Jacqueline J., & Austin, George A. *A study of thinking.* New York: John Wiley and Sons, 1961.

Bruner, Jerome S., Jolly, Alison, & Sylva, Kathy (Eds.). *Play: Its role in development and evolution.* New York: Basic Books, 1976.

Bruyn, Sereryn T. *The human perspective in sociology: The methodology of participant observation.* Englewood Cliffs, New Jersey: Prentice-Hall, 1969.

Buhler, K. *The mental development of the child.* London: Routledge and Kegan Paul, 1930.

Bull, Martha Evans. *The relationship between aural word identification ability and beginning reading performance.* Unpublished doctoral dissertation, Indiana University, 1974.

Bullock, Terry L. *Some psycholinguistic considerations for process and pedagogy in reading. Forum Series of Division of Teacher Education,* 1974, *2.*

Bullowa, Margaret. The acquisition of a word. *Language and Speech,* 1964, *7,* 107-111.

Burke, Carolyn L. The language process: Systems or systematic? In Richard E. Hodges & E. Hugh Rudorf (Eds.), Language and learning to read. Boston: Houghton Mifflin, 1972, 24-31.

Butler, Dorothy, & Clay, Marie. *Reading begins at home.* Auckland, New Zealand: Heinemann Educational Books, 1979.

Calfee, R.C., Chapman, R.S., & Venezky, R.L. How a child needs to think to learn to read. In L.W. Gregg (Ed.), Cognition in learning and memory. New York: John Wiley, 1972, 139-182.

Campbell, Donald T. Degrees of freedom and the case study. *Comparative Political Studies,* 1975, *8,* 178-193.

Campbell, Donald T. The social scientist as methodological servant of the experimenting society. *Policy Studies Journal,* 1973, *2,* 72-75.

Carini, Patricia F. *Observation and description: An alternative methodology for the investigation of human phenomena.* Grand Forks, North Dakota: University of North Dakota Press, 1975.

Carlson, Patricia, & Anisfeld, Moshe. Some observations on the linguistic competence of a two year old child. *Child Development,* 1969, *40,* 569-575.

Carmichael, L. The early growth of language capacity in the individual. In Eric H. Lenneberg (Ed.), *New directions in the study of language.* Cambridge, Massachusetts: MIT press, 1964, 1-22.

Carroll, J.B., & Freedle, R.O. *Language comprehension and the acquisition of knowledge.* Washington, D.C.: V.H. Winston, 1972.

Carroll, John B. *Language and thought.* Englewood Cliffs, New Jersey: Prentic-Hall, 1964.

Carroll, John B. The nature of the reading process. In doris V. Gunderson (Comp.), *Language and reading: An interdisciplinary approach.* Washington, D.C.: Center for Applied Linguistics, 1970, 26-36.

Carroll, John B. Review of Söderbergh's "Reading in early childhood." *Contemporary Society,* 1973, *18,* 33.

Carroll, John B. Some neglected relationships in reading and language learning. *Elementary English,* 1966, *43,* 577-582.

Carroll, John B. Words, meanings, and concepts. In Janet A. Emig (Ed.), *Language and learning.* New York: Harcourt Brace Jovanovich, 1966, 73-101.

Cattell, P. *The measurement of intelligence of infants and young children.* New York: Psychological Corporation, 1960.

Cazden, C., John, V., & Hymes, D. (Eds.). *Functions of language in the classroom.* New York: Teachers College Press, 1972.

Cazden, Courtney B. *Child language and education.* New York: Holt, Rinehart and Winston, 1972.

Cazden, Courtney B. *Environmental assistance to the child's acquisition of grammar.* Unpublished doctoral dissertation, Harvard University, 1965.

Cazden, Courtney B. The neglected situation in child language research and education. In Frederick Williams (Ed.), *Language and poverty.* Chicago: Markham Publishing, 1970, 81-101.

Cazden, Courtney B. On individual differences in language competence and performance. *Journal of Special Education,* 1966, *1,* 135-150.

Cazden, Courtney B. Some implications of research on language development for preschool education. In R.D. Hess & R.M. Bear (Eds.), *Early Education.* Chicago: Aldine, 1968, 131-142.

Cazden, Courtney B. Suggestions from studies of early language acquisition. *Childhood Education,* 1969, *45,* 127-131.

Cazden, Courtney B. (Ed.). *Language in early childhood education.* Washington, D.C.: National Association for the Education of Young Children, 1972.

Cazden, Courtney, & Brown, Roger. The early development of the mother tongue. In Eric W. Lenneberg & Elizabeth Lenneberg (Eds.), *Foundations of language development: A multidisciplinary approach 1.* New York: Academic Press, 1975, 299-309.

Chafe, Wallace L. *Meaning and the structure of language.* Chicago: University of Chicago Press, 1970.

Chomsky, Carol. *Approaching reading through invented spelling.* Paper presented at the Conference on Theory and Practice of Beginning Reading Instruction, Learning Research and Development Center, University of Pittsburgh, 1976.

Chomsky, Carol. How sister got into the grog. *Early Years,* 1975, *6,* 36-39, 78.

Chomsky, Carol. Reading, writing, and phonology. *Harvard Educational Review,* 1970, *40,* 287-309.

Chomsky, Carol. Stages in language development and reading exposure. *Harvard Educational Review,* 1972, *42,* 1-33.

Chomsky, Carol. Write first, read later. *Childhood Education,* 1971, *47,* 296-299.

Chomsky, Carol. Write now, read later. In Courtney B. Cazden (Ed.), *Language in early childhood education.* Washington, D.C.: National Association for the Education of Young Children, 1972, 119-130.

Chomsky, Noam. *Aspects of the theory of syntax.* Cambridge, Massachusetts: MIT Press, 1965.

Chomsky, Noam. *Language and mind.* New York: Harcourt Brace Jovanovich, 1968.

Chukovsky, K. *From two to five.* Berkeley: University of California Press, 1966.

Church, Joseph. *Language and the discovery of reality.* New York: Random House, 1961.

Cicourel, A. The acquisition of social structure: Towards a developmental theory of language and meaning. In J. Douglas (Ed.), *Understanding everyday life.* Chicago: Aldine, 1970.

Clark, Eve V. Knowledge, context, and strategy in the acquisition of meaning. In Daniel P. Dato (Ed.), Developmental psycholinguistics: Theory and application. Washington, D.C.: Georgetown University, 1975, 77-98.

Clark, Eve V. Some aspects of the conceptual basis for first language acquisition. In Richard L. Schiefelbusch & Lyle L. Lloyd (Eds.), *Language Perspectives-acquisition, retardation, and intervention.* Baltimore: University Park Press, 1974, 105-128.

Clark, Eve V. What's in a word? On the child's acquisition of semantics in his first language. In Timothy E. Moore (Ed.), *Cognitive development and the acquisition of language.* New York: Academic Press, 1973, 65-110.

Clark, H., & Lucy, P. Understanding what is meant from what is said: A study in conversationally conveyed requests. *Journal of Verbal Learning and Verbal Behavior,* 1975, *14,* 56-72.

Clark, Margaret M. *Young fluent readers.* London: Heinemann Educational Books, 1976.

Clark, Ruth. What's the use of invitation? *Journal of Child Language,* 1977, *4,* 341-358.

Clarke-Stewart, Alison. *Interactions between mothers and their young children.* Chicago: University of Chicago Press, 1973.

Clay, Marie M. Exploring with a pencil. *Theory into practice,* 1977, *16,* 334-341.

Clay, Marie M. *Reading: The patterning of complex behavior.* Auckland, New Zealand: Heinemann Educational Books, 1972.

Clay, Marie M. *What did I write?* Auckland, New Zealand: Heinemann Educational Books, 1975.

Cohan, Mayme. Two and a half and reading. *Elementary English,* 1961, *38,* 506-508, 517.

Cohen, Dorothy H., & Stern, Virginia. *Observing and recording the behavior of young children.* New York: Teachers College Press, 1978.

Cohn, Margot. Observations of learning to read and write naturally. *Language Arts,* 1981, *58,* 549-555.

Cole, Peter, & Morgan, Jerry L. (Eds.). *Syntax and semantics, vol. 3: Speech acts.* New York: Academic Press, 1975.

Cook-Gumperz, Jenny. The child as practical reasoner. In Mary Sanchez & Ben Blount (Eds.), *Sociocultural dimensions of language use.* New York: Academic Press, 1975, 137-162.

Cook-Gumperz, Jenny, & Corsaro, William A. Socioecological constraints on children's communicative strategies. *Sociology,* 1977, *11,* 411-434.

Cook-Gumperz, Jenny, & Gumperz, John J. Context in children's speech. In working paper #46 *Language and content.* Berkeley: University of California, 1976.

Cooley, Charles H. A study of the early use of self-words by a child. *Psychological Review,* 1908, *15,* 339-357.

Condon, J.C. *Semantics and communication.* New York: Macmillan, 1966.

Cooper, Z. Charlene. *Preschool development of reading, writing, and spelling skills: A case study.* Unpublished master's project, West Virginia College of Graduate Studies, 1981.

Corsaro, William A. The clarification request as a feature of adult interactive styles with young children. *Language in Society,* 1977, *6,* 183-207.

Corsaro, William A. *A developmental sociolinguistic approach to socialization.* Unpublished doctoral dissertation, University of North Carolina at Chapel Hill, 1974.

Coxon, Mary Lukens. Learning to read is doing what comes naturally. In Malcolm P. Douglass (Ed.), *The person in a mass society.* Claremont, California: Claremont College, 1972, 162-167.

Crick, Malcolm. *Explorations in language and meaning.* London: Malaby Press, 1976.

Cromer, R. *The development of temporal references during the acquisition of language.* Unpublished doctoral dissertation, Harvard University, 1968.

Cronbach, Lee J. Beyond the two disciplines of scientific psychology. *American Psychologist,* 1975, *30,* 116-127.

Crystal, David. *Child language, learning, and linguistics.* London: Edward Arnold, 1976.

Dale, Philip S. *Language development.* Hinsdale, Illinois: Dryden Press, 1972.

Darwin, Charles. A biographical sketch of an infant. *Mind,* 1877, *2,* 285-294.

Davis, E.A. The form and function of children's questions. *Child Development,* 1932, *3,* 57-74.

Davis, Fred. The Martian and the convert: Ontological polarities in social reseach. *Urban Life and Culture,* 1973, *2,* 333-343.

Davis, Frederick B. Fundamental factors of comprehension in reading. *Psychometrika,* 1944, *9,* 185-200.

Day, H.I., Berlyne, D.E., & Hunt, D.E. *Intrinsic motivation: A new direction in education.* Minneapolis: Winston Press, 1971.

de Ajuriaguerra, J., & Auzias, M. Preconditions for the development of writing in the child. In Eric H. Lenneberg & Elizabeth Lenneberg (Eds.), *Foundations of language development II.* New York: Academic Press, 1975, 311-328.

De Cecco, J.P. (Ed.). *The psychology of language, thought, and instruction.* New York: Holt, Rinehart and Winston, 1967.

Deese, James. *Psycholinguistics.* Boston: Allyn and Bacon, 1970.

Denzin, Norman K. The genesis of self in early childhood. *Sociological Quarterly,* 1972, *13,* 291-314.

Denzin, Norman K. The logic of naturalistic inquiry. *Social Forces,* 1971, *50,* 166-182.

De Stefano, Johanna. Some parameters of register in adult and child speech. *Review of the Institute of Applied Linguistics,* 1972, *18.*

De Stefano, Johanna S., & Fox, Sharon E. (Eds.). *Language and the language arts.* Boston: Little, Brown, 1974.

de Villiers, Jill G., & de Villiers, Peter A. *Language acquisition.* Cambridge, Massachusetts: Harvard University Press, 1978.

de Villiers, P.A., & de Villiers, J.G. Early judgments of semantic and syntactic acceptability by children. *Journal of Psycholinguistic Research,* 1972, *1,* 299-310.

De Vito, Joseph A. *The psychology of speech and language.* New York: Random House, 1970.

Diesing, Paul. *Patterns of discovery in the social sciences.* Chicago: Aldine-Atherton, 1971.

Dimitrovsky, Lilly, & Almy, Millie. Language and thought: The relationship between knowing a correct answer and ability to verbalize the reasoning on which it is based. *Journal of Psychology,* 1972, *80,* 15-28.

Dittman, A. Developmental factors in conversational behavior. *Journal of Communication,* 1972, *22,* 404-433.

Divita, Ramona. *Teaching a two year old to read: A case study.* Unpublished master's project, West Virginia College of Graduate Studies, 1980.

Doman, Glenn. *How to teach your baby to read.* New York: Random House, 1964.

Donaldson, M., & McGarrigle, J. Some clues to the nature of semantic development. *Journal of Child Language,* 1974, *1,* 185-194.

Dore, John. Children's illocutionary acts. In Roy O. Freedle (Ed.), *Discourse production and comprehension I.* Norwood, New Jersey: Ablex, 1977, 227-244.

Dore, John. Holophrases, speech acts, and language universals. *Journal of Child Language,* 1975, *2,* 21-40.

Dore, John. A pragmatic description of early language development. *Journal of Psycholinguistic Research,* 1974, *4,* 343-350.

Dore, John. Review of Halliday's *Learning how to mean. Language in Society,* 1977, *6,* 114-118.

Doughty, Peter, Pearce, John, & Thorton, Geoffrey. *Exploring language.* London: Edward Arnold Publishers, 1972.

Downing, John. Children's concepts of language in learning to read. *Educational Research,* 1970, *12,* 106-112.

Downing, John. Children's developing concepts of spoken and written language. *Journal of Reading Behavior,* 1971-1972, *4,* 1-19.

Downing, John. The development of linguistic concepts in children's thinking. *Research in the Teaching of English,* 1970, *4,* 5-19.

Downing, John. How children think about reading. *Reading Teacher,* 1969, *23,* 217-230.

Downing, John. The implications of research on children's thinking for the early stages of learning to read. In Malcolm P. Douglass (Ed.), *Self and society*. Claremont, California: Claremont College, 1968, 206-212.

Downing, John. The reading instruction register. *Language Arts,* 1976, *53,* 762-766.

Drach, K. The language of the parent: A pilot study. In working paper +14 *The structure of linguistic input to children.* Language Behavior Research Laboratory, University of California at Berkeley, 1969.

Duckworth, Eleanor. Language and though. In Milton Schwebel & Jane Raph (Eds.), *Piaget in the classroom.* New York: Basic Books, 1973, 132-154.

Durkin, Dolores. Children who learned to read at home. *Elementary School Journal,* 1961, *62,* 15-18.

Durkin, Dolores. Children who read before grade 1: A second study. *Elementary School Journal,* 1963, *64,* 143-148.

Durkin, Dolores. *Children who read early.* New York: Teachers College Press, 1966.

Durkin, Dolores. An earlier start in reading? *Elementary School Journal,* 1962, *63,* 147-151.

Durkin, Dolores. Facts about prefirst grade reading. In Lloyd O. Ollila (Ed.), *The kindergarten child and reading.* Newark, Delaware: International Reading Association, 1977, 1-12.

Durkin, Dolores. A language arts program for prefirst grade children: Two year achievement report. *Reading Research Quarterly,* 1970, *5,* 534-565.

Durkin, Dolores. A six-year study of children who learned to read in school at the age of four. *Reading Research Quarterly,* 1974-1975, *10,* 9-61.

Durkin, Dolores. *Teaching young children to read.* Boston: Allyn & Bacon, 1972.

Durkin, Dolores. What is the value of the new interest in reading comprehension? *Language Arts,* 1981, *58,* 23-43.

Ecroyd, D.H. The relevance of oral language development to classroom teaching. *Today's Speech,* 1973, *21,* 11-19.

Edmonds, Marilyn H. New directions in theories of language acquisition. *Harvard Educational Review,* 1976, *46,* 175-198.

Ehri, Linnea C. Word consciousness in readers and prereaders. *Journal of Educational Psychology,* 1975, *67,* 204-212.

Eimas, P.D., Siqueland, E.R., Jusczyk, P., & Vigorito, J. Speech perception in infants. *Science,* 1971, *171,* 303-306.

Eisner, Elliot W. *Reading the arts, and the creation of meaning.* Reston, Virginia: National Art Education Association, 1978.

Ekwall, Eldon E. *Psychological factors in the teaching of reading.* Columbus, Ohio: Charles E. Merrill, 1973.

Elkind, David. *Children and adolescents: Interpretive essays on Jean Piaget.* New York: o.u.p., 1974.

Elkind, David. Cognitive development and reading. In Malcolm P. Douglass (Ed.), *Reading, thought, and language.* Claremont, California: Claremont College, 1974, 10-20.

Elliott, Lee. Montessori's reading principles involving sensitive period method compared to reading principles of contemporary reading specialists. *Reading Teacher,* 1967, *21,* 163-168.

Emans, Robert. Oral language and learning to read. *Elementary English,* 1973, *50,* 929-934.

Emery, Donald G. *Teach your preschooler to read.* New York: Simon and Schuster, 1975.

Emig, Janet A., Fleming, James T., & Popp, Helen M. *Language and learning.* New York: Harcourt Brace Jovanovich, 1966.

Eng, Helga. *The psychology of child and youth drawing.* New York: Humanities Press, 1957.

Eng, Helga. *The psychology of children's drawings.* London: Routledge and Kegan Paul, 1931.

Entwisle, Doris R. Semantic systems of children: Some assessments of social class and ethnic differences. In Frederick Williams (Ed.), *Language and poverty.* Chicago: Markham Publishing, 1970, 123-152.

Entwisle, Doris R. Young children's expectations for reading. In John T. Guthrie (Ed.), Aspects of reading acquisition. Baltimore: Johns Hopkins Press, 1976, 37-88.

Ervin-Tripp, Susan M. An analysis of the interaction of language, topic, and listener. *American Anthropologist,* 1964, *66,* 86-102.

Ervin-Tripp, Susan M. Imitation and structural change in children's language. *Language acquisition and communicative choice.* Stanford: Stanford University Press, 1973, 185-203.

Ervin-Tripp, Susan M. Is second language learning like the first. *TESOL Quarterly* 1974, *8,* 111-127.

Ervin-Tripp, Susan M. Some strategies for the first two years. In Timothy E. Moore (Ed.), *Cognitive development and the acquisition of language.* New York: Academic Press, 1973a, 261-286.

Ervin-Tripp, Susan M. Structure and process in language acquisition. *Language acquisition and communicative choice.* Stanford: Stanford University Press, 1973, 92-129.

Escalona, S.K. Basic modes of social interaction: Their emergence and patterning during the first two years of life. *Merrill-Palmer Quarterly,* 1973, *19,* 205-232.

Eveloff, Herbert H. Some cognitive and affective aspects of early language development. *Child Development,* 1971, *42,* 1895-1907.

Feffer, M.H. A developmental analysis of interpersonal behavior. *Psychological Review,* 1970, *77,* 197-214.

Feldman, Carol Fleisher. Two functions of language. *Harvard Educational Review,* 1977, *47,* 282-293.

Ferguson, C., & Snow, C. *Talking to children: Language input and acquistion.* New York: Cambridge University Press, 1977.

Ferguson, C.A. Baby talk in six languages. *American Anthropologist,* 1964, *66,* 103-114.

Fillmore, C.J. The case for case. In E. Bach & R.T. Harms (Eds.), *Universals in linguistic theory.* New York: Holt, Rinehart and Winston, 1968, 1-88.

Fillmore, Charles J., Lakoff, George, & Lakoff, Robin (Eds.). *Berkeley studies in syntax and semantics I.* University of California at Berkeley, Institute of Human Learning and Department of Linguistics, 1974.

Finn, Jeremy D. Patterns in children's language. *School Review,* 1969, *77,* 108-127.

Fishbein, Justin, & Emans, Robert. *A question of competence: Language, intelligence, and learning to read.* Chicago: Science Research Associates, 1972.

Fisher, Mary Shattuck. *Language patterns of preschool children.* New York: Teachers College Press, 1934.

Flapan, D. *Children's understanding of social interaction.* New York: Teachers College Press, 1968.

Fowler, William. Teaching a two year old to read: An experiment in early childhood learning. *Genetic Psychology Monographs,* 1962, *66,* 181-283.

Francis, Hazel. Children's experience of reading and notions of units in language. *British Journal of Educational Psychology,* 1973, *43,* 17-23.

Francis, Hazel. *Language in childhood.* New York: St. Martin's Press, 1975.

Francis, Hazel. Linguistic competence and natural language. *La Linguistique,* 1970, *6,* 47-51.

Francis, Hazel. Sentence structure and learning to read. *British Journal of Educational Psychology,* 1972, *42,* 113-119.

Francis, Hazel. Structure in the speech of 2 1/2 year old. *British Journal of Educational Psychology,* 1969, *39,* 291-302.

Fraser, Colin, & Roberts, Naomi. Mothers' speech to children of four different ages. *Journal of Psycholinguistic Research,* 1975, *4,* 9-16.

Freshour, Frank W. Parent education and reading readiness and achievement. *Reading Teacher,* 1971, *24,* 763, 769.

Friedlander, B.Z., Jacobs, A.C., Davis, B.B., & Wetstone, H.S. Time sampling analysis of infants' natural language environments in the home. *Child Development,* 1972, *43,* 730-740.

Garnica, O.K., & Kings, M.L. (Eds.). *Language, children, and society.* New York: Pergamon Press, 1979.

Garvey, C., & Hogan, R. Social speech and social interaction: Egocentrism revisited. *Child Development,* 1973, *44,* 562-568.

Gates, Arthur I. The necessary mental age for beginning reading. *Elementary School Journal,* 1937, *37,* 497-508.

Geest, Ton van der. *The child's communicative competence.* The Hague: Mouton, 1972.

Geest, Ton van der. *Evaluation of theories on child grammar.* The Hague: Mouton, 1974.

Geest, Ton van der. *Some aspects of communicative competence and their implications for language acquisition.* Assen: Van Gorcum, 1975.

Gentry, Richard. Early spelling strategies. *Elementary School Journal,* 1978, *79,* 88-92.

Gentry, Richard. Learning to spell developmentally. *Reading Teacher,* 1981, *34,* 378-381.

Gibson, Eleanor J., & Levin, Harry. *The psychology of reading.* Cambridge, Massachusetts: MIT Press, 1975.

Gibson, Elearnor J., Pick, A., Osser, H., & Hammond, M. The role of grapheme-phoneme correspondence in the perception of words. *American Journal of Psychology,* 1962, *75,* 554-570.

Gilbert, D.C. The young child's awareness of affect. *Child Development,* 1969, *40,* 629-640.

Gillooly, W.B. The influence of writing system characteristics on learning to read. *Reading Research Quarterly,* 1975, *8,* 167-199.

Glass, Gene V. The wisdom of scientific inquiry on education. *Journal of Research in Science Teaching,* 1972, *9,* 3-18.

Gleason, Jean Berko. Code switching in children's language. In Timothy Moore (Ed.), *Cognitive development and the acquisition of language.* New York: Academic Press, 1973, 159-167.

Gleason, Jean Berko. Fathers and other strangers: Men's speech to young children. In Daniel P. Dato (Ed.), *Developmental psycholinguistics: Theory and application.* Washington, D.C.: Georgetown University, 1975, 289-297.

Gleason, Jean Berko, & Weintraub, Sandra. The acquisition of routines in child language. *Language in Society,* 1976, *5,* 129-136.

Gleitman, H., Gleitman, L.R., & Shipley, E. The emergence of the child as grammarian. *Cognition,* 1972, *1,* 137-164.

Glucksberg, Sam., & Danks, Joseph H. *Experimental psycholinguistics.* New York: John Wiley and Sons, 1975.

Goffin, Stacie. Personal conversation. Charleston, West Virginia, 1981.

Goffman, Erving. *Interaction ritual.* Chicago: Aldine Publishing, 1967.

Goffman, Erving. The neglected situation. *American Anthropologist,* 1964, *66,* 133-136.

Goldman, Richard, Peck, Johanne, & Lehane, Stephen. *Looking at children: Field experience in child study.* Atlanta: Humanics Limited, 1976.

Good, Carter V. *Introduction to educational research.* New York: Appleton-Century-Crofts, 1959.

Good, Carter V. *The methodology of educational research.* New York: Appleton-Century-Crofts, 1941.

Goodenough, Florence L. Children's drawings. In C. Murchison (Ed.), *A Handbook of child psychology.* Worcester, Massachusetts: Clark University Press, 1931.

Goodenough, Florence L. Studies in the psychology of children's drawings. *Psychological Bulletin,* 1928, *25,* 272-283.

Goodenough, Florence L., & Harris, D.B. Studies in the psychology of children's drawings: II, 1928-1949. *Psychological Bulletin,* 1950, *47,* 369-433.

Goodman, Kenneth S. Behind the eye: What happens in reading. In Harry Singer & Robert B. Ruddell (Eds.), *Theoretical models and processes of reading.* (2nd ed.). Newark, Delaware: International Reading Association, 1976, 470-496.

Goodman, Kenneth S. Comprehension centered reading. In Eldon E. Ekwall (Ed.), *Psychological factors in the teaching of reading.* Columbus, Ohio: Charles E. Merrill, 1973, 292-301.

Goodman, Kenneth S. Do you have to be smart to read? do you have to read to be smart? *Reading Teacher,* 1975, *29,* 625-632.

Goodman, Kenneth S. *Learning to read is natural.* Paper presented at the Conference on Theory and Practice of Beginning Reading Instruction, Pittsburgh, April 13, 1976.

Goodman, Kenneth S. *The psycholinguistic nature of the reading process.* Detroit: Wayne State University Press, 1968.

Goodman, Kenneth S. Psycholinguistic universals in the reading process. In Frank Smith (Comp.), Psycholinguistics and reading. New York: Holt, Rinehart and Winston, 1973, 21-27.

Goodman, Kenneth S. Reading: The key is in children's language. *Reading Teacher,* 1972, *25,* 505-508.

Goodman, Kenneth S. Reading: A psycholinguistic guessing game. In Harry Singer & Robert Ruddell (Eds.), *Theoretical models and processes of reading* (2nd ed.). Newark, Delaware: International Reading Association, 1976, 259-272.

Goodman, Kenneth S., & Fleming, James T. *Psycholinguistics and the teaching of reading.* Newark, Delaware: International Reading Association, 1969.

Goodman, Yetta. *A psycholinguistic description of observed oral reading phenomena in selected young beginning readers.* Unpublished doctoral dissertation, Wayne State University, 1967.

Goodnow, Jacqueline. *Children drawing.* Cambridge: Harvard University Press, 1977.

Gough, Philip B. The limitations of imitation: The problem of language acquisition. In Alexander Frazier (Ed.), *New directions in elementary English.* Champaign, Illinois: National Council of Teachers of English, 1967, 92-109.

Gould, Toni S. *Home guide to early reading.* New York: Walker and Company, 1975.

Goyvaerts, D.L. The acquisition of social roles. In Sinclair Rogers (Ed.), *Children and language.* London: Oxford University Press, 1975, 113-124.

Graham, Frances K., Berman, Phyllis W., & Ernhart, Claire B. Development in preschool children of the ability to copy forms. *Child Development,* 1960, *31,* 339-359.

Grapko, M.F. Children's conversations: A methodological study of children's language and concept development. *Bulletin of Child Study,* 1963, *25,*.

Graves, Donald H. Let children show us how to help them write. *Visible Language,* 1979, *13,* 16-28.

Greenfield, P.M., May, A.A., & Bruner, J.S. *Early words: Language and action in the life of a child.* New York: John Wiley and Sons, 1972.

Greenfield, Patricia Marks, & Smith, Joshua. *The structure of communication in early language development.* New York: Academic Press, 1976.

Guba, Egon G. *Toward a methodology of naturalistic inquiry in educational evaluation.* CSF Monograph Series in Education, 8. Los Angeles: Center for the Study of Evaluation, 1978.

Guthrie, John T. (Ed.). *Aspects of reading acquisition.* Baltimore: Johns Hopkins Press, 1976.

Hacker, Charles J. From schema theory to classroom practice. *Language Arts,* 1980, *57,* 866-871.

Hall, MaryAnne, & Ramig, C. *Linguistic foundations for reading.* Columbus, Ohio: Charles E. Merrill, 1978.

Halliday, M.A.K. *Explorations in the functions of language.* London, Edward Arnold, 1973.

Halliday, M.A.K. Language acquisition and initial literacy. In Malcolm P. Douglass (Ed.), The many facets of reading. Claremont: California: Claremont College, 1971, 63-68.

Halliday, M.A.K. Language and experience. *Educational Review,* 1968, *20,* 95-106.

Halliday, M.A.K. *Language and social man*. London: Longman for the Schools Council, 1974.

Halliday, M.A.K. Language structure and language function. In J. Lyons (Ed.), *New Horizons in linguistics*. Harmondsworth, England: Penguin Books, 1970.

Halliday, M.A.K. Learning how to mean. In Eric H. Lenneberg & Elizabeth Lenneberg (Eds.), *Foundations of language development: A multidisciplinary approach I*. New York: Academic Press, 1975, 239-265.

Halliday, M.A.K. *Learning how to mean*. New York: Elsevier North Holland, 1975b.

Halliday, M.A.K. Relevant models of language. In Sinclair Rogers (Ed.), *Children and language*. London: Oxford University Press, 1975, 53-65.

Halliday, M.A.K. A rich and adaptable instrument. In J.P.B. Allen & S. Pit Corder (Eds.), *The Edinburgh course in applied linguistics I*. London: Oxford University Press, 1973, 58-65.

Halliday, M.A.K. A sociosemiotic perspective on language development. In Lois Bloom (Ed.), *Readings in language development*. New York: John Wiley and Sons, 1978, 256-277.

Halliday, M.A.K., & Hasan, Ruqaiya. *Cohesion in English*. London: Longmans, 1976.

Halliday, M.A.K., McIntosh, Angus, & Strevens, Peter. *The linguistic sciences and language teaching*. London: Longmans, Green, and Company, 1964.

Hardy, William G. *Language, thought, and experience: A tapestry of the dimensions of meaning*. Baltimore: University Park Press, 1978.

Harris, Dale B. *Children's drawings as measures of intellectual maturity*. New York: Harcourt Brace Jovanovich, 1963.

Harriz, Z. Discourse analysis. *Language*, 1952. *28*, 1-30.

Harste, Jerome C. Reading and reality: A sociopsycholinguistic analysis of reading and reading instruction. In James Robinson (Ed.), *Whole language for whole children*. Bloomington: Indiana University School of Education, 1968.

Harste, Jerome C., & Burke, Carolyn L. Toward a sociopsycholinguistic model of reading comprehension. *Viewpoints in Teaching and Learning*, 1978, *54*, 9-34.

Harste, Jerome C., Burke, Carolyn L., & Woodward, Virginia A. Children's language and world: Initial encounters with print. In Judith Langer & M. Trika Smith-Burke (Eds.), *Reader meets author/Bridging the gap*. Newark, Delaware: International Reading Association, 1979.

Harste, Jerome C., & Carey, Robert F. Comprehension as setting. In Robert F. Carey & Jerome C. Harste (Eds.), New Perspectives on comprehension. Bloomington: Indiana University School of Education, 1979.

Hayes, J.R. (Ed.). *Cognition and the development of language*. New York: Wiley, 1970.

Hebb, D.O., Lambert, W.E., & Tucker, G.R. Language, thought and experience. *Modern Language Journal*, 1971, *55*, 212-222.

Henderson, Edmund H., & Beers, James W. (Eds.). *Developmental and cognitive aspects of learning to spell*. Newark, Delaware: International Reading Association, 1980.

Herron, R.E., & Sutton-Smith, B. *Child's play*. New York: John Wiley, 1971.

Hildreth, Gertrude. Developmental sequences in name writing. *Child Development*, 1936, 7, 291-303.

Hildreth, Gertrude. Early writing as an aid to reading. *Elementary English*, 1963, 40, 15-20.

Hill, Mary. Videotape of Diehl infant. Bloomington: Indiana University, 1979.

Hodges, Richard E., & Rudorf, E. Hugh. (Eds.). *Language and learning to read*. Boston: Houghton Mifflin, 1972.

Holdaway, Don. *The foundations of literacy*. Sidney: Ashton Scholastic, 1979.

Holmes, Jack A., & Singer, Harry. Theoretical models and trends toward more basic research in reading. *Review of Educational Research*, 1964, 34, 127-155.

Holzman, M. The use of interrogative forms in verbal interaction of three mothers and their children. *Journal of Psycholinguistic Research*, 1973, 1, 311-336.

Holzman, M. The verbal environment provided by mothers for their young children. *Merrill Palmer Quarterly*, 1974, 20, 31-42.

Hopper, R. Communicative development and children's responses to questions. *Speech Monographs*, 1971, 38, 1-9.

Hopper, R. Expanding the notion of competence. *Speech Teacher*, 1971, 20, 29-35.

Hopper, Robert, & Naremore, Rita C. *Children's speech*. New York: Harper and Row, 1973.

Horn, Jack C. The value of mother's questions. *Psychology Today*, 1978, 46.

Hughes, Felicity. *Reading and writing before school*. London: Jonathan Cape, 1971.

Hunt, J. McV. Experience and the development of motivation: Some reinterpretations. *Childhood Education*, 1960, 31, 489-504.

Hutchinson, Sally. Personal conversation. Charleston, West Virginia, 1981.

Huttenlocher, Janellen. Children's language: Word-phrase relationships. Science, 1964, 143, 264-265.

Huxley, R., & Ingram, E. (Eds.). *Language development: Models and methods*. New York: Academic Press, 1971.

Hymes, Dell. The ethnography of speaking. In T. Gladwin & W.C. Sturtevant (Eds.), *Anthropology and human behavior*. Washington, D.C.: Anthropological Society of Washington, 1962, 13-53.

Hymes, Dell. The functions of speech. In John P. DeCecco (Ed.), *The psychology of language, thought, and instruction*. New York: Holt, Rinehart and Winston, 1967. 103-108.

Hymes, Dell. Models of the interaction of language and social setting. *Journal of Social Issues*, 1967, 23, 8-28.

Hymes, Dell. *On communicative competence*. Philadelphia: University of Pennsylvania, 1971.

Ingram, David. The relationship between comprehension and production. In Richard L. Schiefelbusch & Lyle L. Lloyd (Eds.), *Language perspectives—Acquisition, retardation, and intervention*. Baltimore, Maryland: University Park Press, 1974, 313-334.

Irwin, E.C. Play and language development. *Speech Teacher*, 1975, 24, 15-23.

Jackson, Robert K. Implications of language research for reading teaching. *Reading Improvement,* 1972, *9,* 3-9, 27.

Jencks, Christopher. *Inequality.* New York: Harper and Row, 1972.

Jenkinson, Marion D. Sources of knowledge for theories of reading. In Doris V. Gunderson (Comp.), *Language and reading: an interdisciplinary approach.* Washington, D.C. Center for Applied Linguistics, 1970, 55-71.

Jespersen, Otto. *Language: Its nature, development, and origin.* New York: Holt, Rinehart and Winston, 1922.

Johnson, Marjorie Seddon. Thought-language-reading. *Proceedings of the 1969 annual reading institute.* Philadelphia: Temple University, 1970, 103-108.

Jones, R.M. *System in child language.* Cardiff: University of Wales Press, 1970.

Karpova, Sofja Nikolaevna. *The realization of the verbal composition of speech by preschool children.* The Hague: Mouton, 1977.

Kasdon, Lawrence M. Early reading background of some superior readers among college freshmen. *Journal of Educational Research,* 1958, *52,* 151-153.

Katz, Jerome J., & Fodor, Jerry A. The structure of a semantic theory. *Language,* 1963, *39,* 170-210.

Kavale, Kenneth, & Schriener, Robert. Psycholinguistic implications for beginning reading instruction. *Language Arts,* 1978, *55,* 34-40.

Kavanagh, James F., & Mattingly, Ignatius G. (Eds.), *Language by ear and by eye.* Cambridge: MIT Press, 1972.

Keenan, Elinor O. Conversational competence in children. *Journal of Child Language,* 1974, *1,* 163-183.

Keenan, Elinor O. Review of Halliday's *Explorations in the functions of language. Language in Society,* 1975, *2,* 247-253.

Kellogg, Rhoda. Understanding children's art. *Psychology Today,* 1967, *1,* 16-25.

Kernan, Keith T. Semantic relationships of the child's acquisition of language. *Anthropological Linguistics,* 1970, *12,* 171-187.

King, E.M., & Friesen, D.T. Children who read in kindergarten. *Alberta Journal of Educational Research,* 1972, *18,* 147-161.

King, Martha, & Rentel, Victor. Toward a theory of early writing development. *Research in the Teaching of English,* 1979, *13,* 243-253.

Kobashigawa, B. *Repetitions in a mother's speech in her child.* Working paper #14. Berkeley: University of California, 1969.

Kohl, Herbert. *Reading: How to.* New York: E.P. Dutton, 1973.

Kolers, Paul A. Reading is only incidentally visual. In Kenneth S. Goodman & James T. Fleming (Eds.), *Psycholinguistics and the teaching of reading.* Newark, Delaware: International Reading Association, 1969, 8-16.

Koppenhaver, Albert H. Reading in the home environment. In Malcolm P. Douglass (Ed.), *Reading, thought, and language.* Claremont, California: Claremont College, 1974, 122-129.

Krauss, R.M., & Glucksberg, S. The development of communicative competence as a function of age. *Child Development,* 1969, *40,* 255-266.

Krippener, Stanley. The boy who read at eighteen months. *Exceptional Children,* 1963, *30,* 105-109.

Labov, William, & Waletzky, Joshua. Narrative analysis: Oral versions of personal experience. *Essays on the verbal and visual arts.* Seattle: University of Washington Press, 1967, 12-45.

LaConte, Christine. Reading in kindergarten. *Reading Teacher,* 1969, *23,* 116-120.

LaCrosse, E. Robert, Jr. Reading readiness in the preschool years: A total preparation by the environment. In Malcolm P. Douglass (Ed.), *The many facets of reading.* Claremont, California: Claremont College, 1971.

Lakoff, Robin. Language in context. *Language,* 1972, *48,* 907-927.

Langer, Susanne K. *Feeling and form.* New York: Charles Scribner's Sons, 1953.

Lavine, L.O. *The development of perception of writing in prereading children: A cross-cultural study.* Unpublished doctoral dissertation, Cornell University, 1972.

Lee, D., & Allen, R.V. *Learning to read through experience.* New York: Appleton-Century-Crofts, 1963.

Legrun, A. Wie and was 'Schreiben' kindergarten zöglinge? *Seitschrift fur Padogogische Psychologie,* 1932, *33,* 322-331.

Lenneberg, Eric H. *The biological foundations of language.* New York: Wiley, 1967.

Lenneberg, Eric H. On explaining language. In Doris V. Gunderson (Comp.), *Language and reading: An interdisciplinary approach.* Washington, D.C.: Center for Applied Linguistics, 1970, 1-25.

Lenneberg, Eric H. (Ed.). *New directions in the study of language.* Cambridge, Massachusetts: MIT Press, 1968.

Lenneberg, Eric H., & Lenneberg, Elizabeth. *Foundations of language development: A multidisciplinary approach.* New York: Academic Press, 1975.

Leonard, L.B. *Meaning in child language.* New York: Grune and Stratton, 1976.

Leopold, Werner F. Patterning in children's language learning. *Language Learning,* 1953-1954, *5,* 1-4.

Leopold, Werner F. *Speech development of a bilingual child. A linguist's record, III: Grammar and general problems in the first two years.* Evanston, Illinois: Northwestern University Press, 1949.

Levine, Murray. Scientific method and the adversary model. *American Psychologist,* 1974, 661-667.

Lewis, M.M. *How children learn to speak.* New York: Basic Books, 1959.

Lewis, M.M. *Infant speech.* New York: Humanities Press, 1951.

Lewis, M.M. *Language and the child.* London: King, Thorne and Stace, 1969.

Lewis, M.M. Language and exploration. In Sinclair Rogers (Ed.), *Children and language.* London: Oxford University Press, 1975, 153-172.

Lewis, M.M. *Language in society.* New York: Social Sciences Publishers, 1948.

Lewis, M.M. *Language, thought, and personality.* New York: Basic Books, 1963.

Lewis, Michael, & Freedle, Roy. Mother-infant dyad: The cradle of meaning. In P. Pliner, L. Krames, & T. Alloway (Eds.), *Communication and affect: Language and thought.* New York: Academic Press, 1973, 127-154.

Lewis, Michael, & Rosenblum, Leonard A. *The effect of the infant on its caregiver.* New York: John Wiley and Sons, 1974.

Lillard, Paula Polk. *Montessori: A modern approach.* New York: Schocken Books, 1972.

Lock, Andrew (Ed.). *Action, gesture, and symbol: The emergence of language.* London: Academic Press, 1978.

Lotz, John. How language is conveyed by script. In James F. Kavanagh & Ignatius G. Mattingly (Eds.), *Language by ear and by eye.* Cambridge, Massachusetts: MIT Press, 1972.

Lutz, Frank, & Ramsey, Margaret A. The use of anthropological field methods in education. *Educational Researcher,* 1974, *3,* 5-9.

Mackintosh, Helen K. *Children and oral language.* ACEI, ASCD, IRA, NCTE, 1964.

Mackworth, J.F. Some models of the reading process: Learners and skilled readers. *Reading Research Quarterly,* 1972, *7,* 701-733.

Mackworth, N.H., & Bruner, J.S. How adults and children search and recognize pictures. *Human Development,* 1970, *13,* 149-177.

Macnamara, John. Cognitive basis of language learning. *Psychological Review,* 1972, *79,* 1-13.

Marge, M. The influence of selected home background variables on the development of oral communication skills in children. *Journal of Speech and Hearing Research,* 1965, *8,* 291-309.

Markova, Ivana. *The social context of language.* New York: John Wiley and Sons, 1978.

Martlew, Margaret, Connolly, Kevin, & McCleod, Christine. Language use, role and context in a five year old. *Journal of Child Language,* 1978, *5,* 81-99.

Mason, J. When do children begin to read: An exploration of four year old children's letter and word reading comprehension. *Reading Research Quarterly,* 1980, *15,* 203-227.

Mason, George. Preschoolers' concepts of reading. *Reading Teacher,* 1967, *21,* 130-132.

Mass, L. *Developing concepts of literacy in young children.* Paper presented at Symposium 47, International Reading Association Convention, New Orleans, April 1981.

May, Frank B. The effects of environment on oral language development: I. Home environment. *Elementary English,* 1966, *43,* 587-595.

McCarthy, Dorothea. Language development in children. In Leonard Carmichael (Ed.), *Manual of child psychology.* New York: John Wiley and Sons, 1954, 492-630.

McCarthy, Dorothea. *The language development of the preschool child.* Minneapolis: University of Minnesota Press, 1930.

McCracken, Robert A. A two year study of the reading achievement of children who were reading when they entered first grade. *Journal of Educational Research,* 1966, *59,* 207-210.

McDermott, R.P. The cultural context of learning to read. In Stanley F. Wanat (Ed.), *Issues in evaluating reading.* Arlington, Virginia: Center for Applied Linguistics, 1977, 10-18.

McElroy, C.W. *Speech and language development of the preschool child: A survey.* Springfield, Illinois: Charles C. Thomas, 1972.

McKenzie, Moira. The beginnings of literacy. *Theory into practice,* 1977, *16,* 315-323.

McKenzie, Moira. *The range of operative structure underlying the behavior of young readers and nonreaders engaged in reading and writing activities.* Unpublished doctoral dissertation, Ohio State University, 1974.

McLean, James E., & Snyder-McLean, Lee K. *A transactional approach to early language training.* Columbus, Ohio: Charles E. Merrill, 1978.

McNeill, David. *The acquisition of language.* New York: Harper and Row, 1970.

Medinnus, Gene R. *Child study and observation guide.* New York: John Wiley and Sons, 1976.

Menyuk, Paula. *Acquisition and development of language.* Englewood Cliffs, New Jersey: Prentice-Hall, 1971.

Menyuk, Paula. Early development of receptive language: From babbling to words. In Richard L. Schiefelbusch & Lyle L. Lloyd (Eds.), *Language perspectives-acquisition, retardation, and intervention.* Baltimore: University Park Press, 1974, 213-235.

Menyuk, Paula. *Language and maturation.* Cambridge, Massachusetts: MIT Press, 1977.

Menyuk, Paula. Language theories and educational practices. In Frederick Williams (Ed.), *Language and poverty.* Chicago: Markham Publishing, 1970, 190-211.

Menyuk, Paula. A preliminary evaluation of grammatical capacity in children. *Journal of Verbal Learning and Verbal Behavior,* 1963, *2,* 429-439.

Menyuk, Paula. *Sentences children use.* Cambridge, Massachusetts: MIT Press, 1969.

Miel, Alice (Ed.). *Individualizing reading practices.* New York: Teachers College Press, 1958.

Millar, S. *The psychology of play.* Baltimore: Penguin Books, 1969.

Miller, Edith, & Warner, Richard W. Single subject research and evaluation. *Personnel and Guidance Journal,* 1975, *57,* 130-133.

Miller, George A. *Spontaneous apprentices: Children and language.* New York: Continuum Book, 1977.

Miller, Wilma H. Certain home environmental factors and children's reading readiness. In Carl Braun (Ed.), *Language, reading, and the communication process.* Newark, Delaware: International Reading Association, 1971, 167-172.

Milner, Esther. A study of the relationship between reading readiness in grade one school children and patterns of parent-child interaction. *Child Development,* 1951, *22,* 95-112.

Minifie, F.D., & Lloyd, L.L. (Eds.), *Communicative and cognitive abilities: Early behavior assessment.* Baltimore: University Park Press, 1977.

Mishler, Elliot G. Meaning in context: Is there any other kind? *Harvard Educational Review,* 1979, *49,* 1-19.

Mitchell-Kernan, C., & Ervin-Tripp, S. (Eds.). *Child discourse.* New York: Academic Press, 1977.

Moerk, Ernst. Principles of interaction in language learning. *Merrill Palmer Quarterly,* 1972, *18,* 229-257.

Moffett, James, & Wagner, Betty Jane. *Student-centered language arts and reading, K-13.* (2nd. ed.). New York: Houghton Mifflin, 1976.

Morehead, Donald M., & Morehead, Ann. From signal to sign: A Piagetian view of thought and language during the first two years. In Richard L. Schiefelbusch & Lyle L. LLoyd (Eds.), *Language perspectives-acquisition, retardation, and intervention.* Baltimore: University Park Press, 1974, 153-189.

Morimoto, Kiyo. Notes on the context for learning. *Harvard Educational Review,* 1973, *43,* 245-257.

Morris, D. *The biology of art.* New York: Knopf, 1962.

Mowrer, O. Hobart *Learning theory and the symbolic processes.* New York: Wiley, 1960.

Mowrer, O. Hobart. The psychologist looks at language. *American Psychologist,* 1954, *9,* 660-694.

Mueller, E.C. *An analysis of children's communications in free play.* Unpublished doctoral dissertation, Cornell University, 1971.

Mueller, E.C. The maintenance of verbal exchanges between young children. *Child Development,* 1972, *43,* 930-938.

Murray, Frank B. *Reading and understanding.* Newark, Delaware: International Reading Association, 1980.

Nakazima, Sei. Phonemicization and symbolization in language development. In Eric H. Lenneberg & Elizabeth Lenneberg (Eds.), *Foundations of language development: A multidisciplinary approach I.* New York: Academic Press, 1975, 181-187.

Nelson, Katherine. Concept, word, and sentence: Interrelations in acquisition and development. *Psychological Review,* 1974, *81,* 267-285.

Nelson, Katherine. Some evidence for the cognitive primacy of categorization and its functional basis. *Merrill-Palmer Quarterly,* 1973, *19,* 21-39.

Nelson, Katherine. *Structure and strategy in learning to talk. Monographs of the Society for Research in Child Development,* +149, 1973, *38.*

Newport, E.L. *'Motherese': The speech of mothers to young children.* Technical Report +52, Center for Human Information Processing. San Diego: University of California, 1975.

Nice, Margaret Morse. The development of a child's vocabulary in relation to environment. *Pedagogical Seminary,* 1915, *22,* 35-63.

Ninio, Anat, & Bruner, Jerome. The achievements and antecedents of labeling. *Journal of Child Language,* 1978, *5,* 1-15.

Norman, D.A., & Bobrow, D.G. On data limited and resource limited processes. *Cognitive Psychology,* 1975, *7,* 44-64.

Norman, D.A., & Bobrow, D.G. Some preinciples of memory schemata. In D.G. Bobrow & A.M. Collins (Eds.), *Representation and understanding: Studies in cognitive science.* New York: Academic Press, 1975.

Ollila, Lloyd O. (Ed.). *The kindergarten child and reading.* Newark, Delaware: International Reading Association, 1977, 13-39.

Ollila, Lloyd O. Pros and cons of teaching reading to four and five year olds. In Robert C. Aukerman (Ed.), *Some persistent questions on beginning reading.* Newark, Delaware: International Reading Association, 1972, 53-61.

Olim, Ellis G. Maternal language styles and cognitive development of children. In Frederick Williams (Ed.), Language and poverty. Chicago: Markham Publishing, 1970, 212-228.

Oliver, Marvin E. *Making readers of everyone.* Dubuque, Iowa: Kendall/Hunt, 1976.

Olson, David R. From utterance to text: The bias of language in speech and writing. *Harvard Educational Review,* 1977, *47,* 257-281.

Olson, David R. Language and thought: Aspects of a cognitive theory of semantics. *Psychological Review,* 1970, *77,* 257-273.

Osser, Harry. Bilogical and social factors in language. In Frederick Williams (Ed.), *Language and poverty: Perspectives on a theme.* Chicago: Markham Publishing, 1979, 248-264.

Overholt, George E., & Stallings, William M. Ethnographic and experimental hypotheses in educational research. *Educational Researcher,* 1976, *5,* 12-14.

Parisi, Domenico. What is behind child utterances? *Journal of Child Language,* 1974, *1,* 97-105.

Paul, R. Invented spelling in kindergarten. *Young Children,* 1976, *31,* 195-200.

Pflaum, Susanna Whitney. *The development of language and reading in the young child.* Columbus, Ohio: Charles E. Merrill, 1974.

Pflaum-Connor, Susanna (Ed.). *Aspects of reading education.* Berkeley: McCutchan Publishing, 1978.

Phillips, Derek L. *Abandoning method.* San Francisco: Josse-Bass Publishers, 1978.

Phillips, Judith Rapaport. *Formal characteristics of speech which mothers address to their young children.* Unpublished doctoral dissertation, Johns Hopkins University, 1970.

Piaget, Jean. *The construction of reality in the child.* New York: Basic Books, 1954.

Piaget, Jean. *The language and thought of the child.* New York: Humanities Press, 1965.

Piaget, Jean, & Inhelder, Barbel. *The psychology of the child.* New York: Basic Books, 1969.

Pines, Maya. How children learn to talk. *Redbook,* 1979, *35,* 217, 219, 221.

Pines, Maya. How three year olds teach themselves to read—love it. *Harper's Magazine,* 1963, *226,* 58-64.

Pitcher, E., & Prelinger, E. *Children tell stories.* New York: International Universities Press, 1963.

Plessas, Gus P., & Oakes, Clifton R. Prereading experiences of selected early readers. *Reading Teacher,* 1964, *17,* 241-245.

Plinger, P., Krames, L., & Alloway, T. (Eds.). *Communication and affect: Language and thought.* New York: Academic Press, 1973.

Polk, D., & Goldstein, D. Early reading and concrete operations. *Journal of Psychology,* 1980, *106,* 111-116.

Pratt, Mary Louise. *Toward a speech act theory of literary discourse.* Bloomington, Indiana: Indiana University Press, 1977.

Prior, Mary D. Notes on the first three years of a child. *Pedagogical Seminary,* 1894, *3,* 339-341.

Ratner, Nancy, & Bruner, Jerome. Games, social exchange, and the acquisition of language. *Journal of Child Language,* 1978, *5,* 391-401.

Read, Allen Walker. Family language. In Sinclair Rogers (Ed.), *Children and language.* London: Oxford University Press, 1975, 125-134.

Read, Charles. *Children's categorization of speech sounds in English.* Urbana, Illinois: National Council of Teachers of English, 1975.

Read, Charles. Lessons to be learned from the preschool orthographer. In Eric H. Lenneberg & Elizabeth Lenneberg (Eds.), *Foundations of language development II.* New York: Academic Press, 1975, 329-346.

Read, Charles. Preschool children's knowledge of English phonology. *Harvard Educational Review,* 1971, *4,* 1-34.

Reich, Peter A. Early acquisition of word meaning. *Journal of Child Language,* 1976, *3,* 117-123.

Reid, J.F. Learning to think about reading. *Educational Research,* 1966, *9,* 56-62.

Remick, H. *The maternal environment of linguistic development.* Unpublished doctoral dissertation, University of California at Davis, 1971.

Renzuli, J.S. Confessions of a frustrated evaluator. In D. Payne (Ed.), *Curriculum evaluation.* Washington, D.C.: 1974, 49.

Robeck, Mildred C. Affective learning in the language development of young children. *Journal of Research and Development in Education,* 1969, *3,* 32-42.

Robinson, H. Alan. Psycholinguistics, sociolinguistics, reading, and the classroom teacher. In Thomas C. Barrett & Dale D. Johnson (Eds.), *Views of Elementary Reading Instruction.* Newark, Delaware: International Reading Association, 1973, 3-11.

Rodnick, R., & Wood, B. The communication strategies of children. *Reading Teacher,* 1973, *22,* 114-124.

Roeper, Thomas. Connecting children's language and linguistic theory. In Timothy E. Moore (Ed.), *Cognitive development and language acquisition.* New York: Academic Press, 1973, 189-196.

Rogers, Sinclair (Ed.). *Children and language.* London: Oxford University Press, 1975.

Rothney, John W.M. *Methods of studying the individual child.* Waltham, Massachusetts: Blaisdell Publishing, 1968.

Ryan, Ellen Bouchard, & Semmel, Melvyn I. Reading as a constructive language process. *Reading Research Quarterly,* 1969, *5,* 59-83.

Ryan, J. Early language development: Towards a communicational analysis. In P.M. Richards (Ed.), *The integration of the child into a social world.* London: Cambridge University Press, 1974, 185-214.

Ryan, John. Family patterns of reading problems: The family that reads together.... In Malcolm P. Douglass (Ed.), *All things considered.* Claremont, California: Claremont College, 1977, 159-163.

Sachs, Jacqueline, & Devin, Judith. Young children's use of age-appropriate speech styles in social interaction and role playing. *Journal of Child Language,* 1976, *3,* 81-98.

Sadock, Jerrold M. *Toward a linguistic theory of speech acts.* New York: Academic Press, 1974.

Salazin, Susan. Exploring goal-free evaluation: An interview with Michael Scriven. *Evaluation,* 1974, *2,* 9-16.

Samuels, S. Jay. Controversial issues in beginning reading instruction: Meaning versus subskill emphasis. In Susanna Pflaum-Connor (Ed.), *Aspects of reading education.* Berkeley: McCutchan Publishing, 1978, 44-62.

Sander, E.K. How significant is a baby's babbling? *Elementary English,* 1969, *46,* 80-84.

Saporta, Sol (Ed.). *Psycholinguistics: A book of readings.* New York: Holt, Rinehart and Winston, 1961.

Sartain, Harry W. Psychological aspects of reading readiness. *Psychological and physiological aspects of reading.* Pittsburgh: University of Pittsburgh, 1968, 71-80.

Sartain, Harry W. Readiness in the language arts. *Reading and the language arts.* Pittsburgh: University of Pittsburgh, 1965, 29-38.

Savin, H.B., & Bever, T.G. The nonperceptual reality of the phoneme. *Journal of Verbal Learning and Verbal Behavior,* 1970, *9,* 295-302.

Savin, Harris B. What a child knows about speech when he starts to learn to read. In James F. Kavanaugh & Ignatius G. Mattingly (Eds.), *Language by ear and by eye.* Cambridge, Massachusetts: MIT Press, 1972, 319-326.

Schacter, Frances Fuchs. Everyday caretaker talk to toddlers versus threes and fours. *Journal of Child Language,* 1976, *3,* 221-1'245.
language acquisition. *Journal of Child Language,* 1977, *4,* 153-169.

Schacter, Frances Fuchs. *Everyday preschool interpersonal speech usage: Methodological, developmental, and sociolinguistic studies.* Monographs of the Society for Research in Child Development, #156, 1974, *39.*

Schaeffer, H.R. (Ed.). *The origins of human social behaviors.* New York: Academic Press, 1971.

Schiefelbusch, Richard, & Lloyd, Lyle L. (Eds.). *Language perspectives: Acquisition, retardation, and intervention.* Baltimore: University Park Press, 1974.

Schickedanz, Judith A. Hey! This book's not working right. *Young Children,* 1981, 18-27.

Schickedanz, Judith A. Please read that story again! *Young Children,* 1978, 48-55.

Schlesinger, I.M. Grammatical development—the first steps. In Eric H. Lenneberg & Elizabeth Lenneberg (Eds.), *Foundations of language development: A multidisciplinary approach I.* New York: Academic Press, 1975, 203-222.

Schlesinger, I.M. Production of utterances and language acquisition. In D.I. Slobin (Ed.), *The ontogenesis of grammar.* New York: Academic Press, 1971, 63-101.

Schlesinger, I.M. Relational concepts underlying language. In Richard L. Schiefelbusch & Lyle L. Lloyd (Eds.), *Language perspectives—acquisition, retardation, and intervention.* Baltimore: University Park Press, 1974.

Schlesinger, I.M. The role of cognitive development and linguistic input in language acquisition. *Journal of Child Language,* 1977, *4,* 153-169.

Schmidt, W., & Hore, T. Some nonverbal aspects of communication between mother and child. *Child Development,* 1979, *41,* 889-896.

Scollon, Ronald. *Conversations with a one year old.* Honolulu: University Press of Hawaii, 1976.

Searle, J.R. *Speech acts: An essay in the philosophy of language.* New York: Cambridge University Press, 1969.

Shatz, Marilyn. Children's comprehension of their mother's question directives. *Journal of Child Language,* 1978, *5,* 39-46.

Sheldon, William D. Teaching the very young to read. *Reading Teacher,* 1962, *16,* 163-169.

Sheldon, William D., & Carrillo, Lawrence. Relation of parents, home, and certain developmental characteristics to children's reading ability. *Elementary School Journal,* 1952, *52,* 262-270.

Shinn, N.W. *Notes on the development of a child.* Berkeley: University of California, 1893.

Shipley, Elizabeth F., Smith, Carlota S., & Gleitman, Lila R. A study in the acquisition of language: Free responses to commands. *Language,* 1969, *45,* 322-342.

Sinclair, H. The role of cognitive structures in language acquisition. In Eric H. Lenneberg & Elizabeth Lenneberg (Eds.), *Foundations of language development: A multidisciplinary approach I.* New York: Academic Press, 1975, 223-238.

Sinclair-de Zwart, H. Language acquisition and cognitive development. In Timothy E. Moore (Ed.), *Cognitive development and the acquisition of language.* New York: Academic Press, 1973, 9-25.

Singer, Harry. Theoretical models of reading. In Harry Singer & Robert B. Ruddell (Eds.), *Theoretical models and processes of reading.* Newark, Delaware: International Reading Association, 1976, 634-654.

Singer, Harry, & Ruddell, Robert B. (Eds.). *Theoretical models and processes of reading* (2nd ed.). Newark, Delaware: International Reading Association, 1976.

Skinner, B.F. *Verbal behavior.* New York: Appleton-Century-Crofts, 1957.

Slobin, Dan I. *Early grammatical development in several languages, with special attention to Soviet research.* Working Paper #11, Language Behavior Research Laboratory. University of California at Berkeley, 1968a.

Slobin, Dan I. Grammatical transformations in childhood and adulthood. *Journal of Verbal Learning and Verbal Behavior,* 1966, *5,* 219-227.

Slobin, Dan I. *Leopold's bibliography of child language.* Bloomington: Indiana University Press, 1972.

Slobin, Dan I. On the nature of talk to children. In Eric H. Lenneberg & Elizabeth Lenneberg (Eds.), *Foundations of language development: A multidisciplinary approach.* New York: Academic Press, 1975, 283-297.

Slobin, Dan I. *Psycholinguistics.* Glenview, Illinois: Scott, Foresman, 1971.

Slobin, Dan I. Questions of language development in cross-cultural perspective. In Kerry M. Drach (Ed.), *The structure of linguistic input to children.* Working Paper #14, Language-Behavior Research Laboratory, University of California at Berkeley, 1968b.

Slobin, Dan I. *Studies of child language development.* New York: Holt, Rinehart and Winston, 1973.

Slobin, Daniel I., & Welsh, Charles A. Elicited imitations as a research tool in developmental psycholinguistics. In Charles A. Ferguson & Daniel I. Slobin (Eds.), *Studies of child language development.* New York: Holt, Rinehart and Winston, 1973, 170-185.

Smith, Carlota. An experimental approach to children's linguistic competence. In John R. Hayes (Ed.), *Cognition and the development of language,* New York: John Wiley and Sons, 1970, 109-133.

Smith, Frank. *Comprehension and learning.* New York: Holt, Rinehart and Winston, 1975a.

Smith, Frank. Making sense of reading—and of reading instruction. *Harvard Educational Review,* 1977, *47,* 386-395.

Smith, Frank. *Psycholinguistics and reading.* New York: Holt, Rinehart and Winston, 1973.

Smith, Frank. The relation between spoken and written language. In Eric H. Lenneberg & Elizabeth Lenneberg (Eds.), *Foundations of language development II.* New York: Academic Press, 1975b, 347-360.

Smith, Frank. *Understanding reading.* New York: Holt, Rinehart and Winston, 1971.

Smith, Frank, & Miller, George (Eds.). *The genesis of language.* Cambridge, Massachusetts: MIT Press, 1966.

Snow, Catherine E. The development of conversation between mothers and babies. *Journal of Child Language,* 1977, *4,* 1-22.

Snow, Catherine E. *Language acquisition and mothers' speech to children.* Unpublished doctoral dissertation, McGill University, 1971.

Snow, Catherine E. Mothers' speech to children learning language. *Child Development,* 1973, *43,* 549-565.

Snow, Catherine E., & Ferguson, Charles A. *Talking to children.* Cambridge: Cambridge University Press, 1977.

Söderbergh, Ragnhild. Learning to read between two and five: Some observations on normal hearing and deaf children. In Clea Rameh (Ed.), *Semantics: Theory and application. Washington: Georgetown University Press, 1976, 257-279.*

Söderbergh, Ragnhild. *Reading in early childhood: a linguistic study of a Swedish preschool child's gradual acquisition of reading ability.* Stockholm, Sweden: Almquist & Wiksell, 1971.

Söderbergh, Ragnhild. Review article: Language by ear and by eye. *Journal of Child Language,* 1975, *2,* 153-168.

Staats, A.W., & Staats, C. A comparison of the development of speech and reading behavior with implications for research. *Child Development,* 1962, *23,* 831-846.

Staats, Arthur W. Linguistic-mentalistic theory versus an explanatory s-r learning theory of language development. In Dan I. Slobin (Ed.), *The ontogenesis of grammar.* New York: Academic Press, 1971, 103-150.

Stake, Robert E. The case study method in social inquiry. *Educational Researcher,* 1978, *7,* 5-8.

Stemmer, N. Semantic approaches to language acquisition. *Language Sciences,* 1973, *26,* 4-6.

Stern, W. *Psychology of early childhood.* London: Allen & Unwin, 1924.

Strickland, Ruth. Children's language and their reading. In Nila Banton Smith & Ruth Strickland (Eds.), *Some approaches to reading.* Washington, D.C.: Association for Childhood International, 1969.

Strickland, Ruth. *The language and mental development of children. Bulletin of the School of Education, Indiana University,* 1947, *23.*

Sudnow, D. (Ed.), *Studies in social interaction.* New York: Free Press, 1972.

Sully, J. *Studies of childhood.* London: Longmans, 1895.

Sutton, Marjorie Hunt. Children who learned to read in kindergarten: A longitudinal Study. *Reading Teacher,* 1969, *7,* 595-602, 683.

Sutton, Marjorie Hunt. First grade children who learned to read in kindergarten. *Reading Teacher,* 1965, *19,* 192-196.

Taine, H. On the acquisition of language by children. *Mind,* 1877, *2,* 252-259.

Teale, W. Positive environments for learning to read: What studies of early readers tell us. *Language Arts,* 1978, *55,* 922-932.

Terman, Lewis M. An experiment in infant education. *Journal of Applied Psychology,* 1918, *2,* 219-228.

Todd, G., & Palmer, B. Social reinforcement of infant babbling. *Child Development,* 1968, *39,* 591-596.

Torrey, Jane W. Learning to read without a teacher: A case study. In Frank Smith (Ed.), *Psycholinguistics and reading*. New York: Holt, Rinehart and Winston, 1973, 147-157.

Torrey, Jane W. Reading that comes naturally. In Gary T. Waller & G.E. Mac-Kinnon (Eds.), *Reading Research: Advances in theory and practice*, vol. 1. New York: Academic Press, 1979.

Tough, Joan. *The development of meaning: A study of children's use of language*. New York: John Wiley and Sons, 1977.

Umiker-Sebeok, O. Jean Preschool children's intraconversational narratives. *Journal of Child Language,* 1979, *6,* 91-109.

Van der Horst, L. Affect, expression, and symbolic function in the drawing of children. In M.L. Reymert (Ed.), *Feelings and emotions*. New York: McGraw Hill, 1950, 398-417.

Venezky, Richard L., Calfee, Robert C., & Chapman, Robin S. Skills required for learning to read. In Doris V. Gunderson (Comp.), *Language and reading: An interdisciplinary approach*. Washington, D.C.: Center for Applied Linguistics, 1970, 35-54.

Verma, S.K. Towards a linguistic analysis of registral features. *Acta Linguistica Academiae Scientiarum Hungaricae,* 1969, *19,* 293-303.

Vidich, Arthur J. Participant observation and the collection and interpretation of data. *American Journal of Sociology,* 1954, *60,* 354-360.

Vygotsky, Lev. S. *Mind in society*. Cambridge, Massachusetts: Harvard University Press, 1978.

Vygotsky, Lev. S. *Thought and language*. Cambridge, Massachusetts: MIT Press, 1968.

Walden, James (Ed.). *Oral language and reading*. Urbana, Illinois: National Council of Teachers of English, 1969.

Walton, Richard E. Advantages and attributes of the case study. *Journal of Applied Behavioral Science,* 1972, *8,* 73-78.

Wanat, Stanley F. Criteria for evaluating readiness: 'When is a child intelligent enough to read?' In Stanley F. Wanat (Ed.), *Issues in evaluating reading*. Arlington, Virginia: Center for Applied Linguistics, 1977a, 19-27.

Wanat, Stanley F. Developmental psycholinguistics: Implications for reading research. In Stanley F. Wanat (Ed.), *Language and reading comprehension*. Arlington, Virginia: Center for Applied Linguistics, 1977b, 36-42.

Ward, Evangeline. A child's first reading teacher: His parents. *Reading Teacher,* 1970, *23,* 756-759.

Warden, D.A. The influence of context on children's use of identifying expressions and references. *British Journal of Psychology,* 1976, *67,* 101-112.

Wardhaugh, Ronald. *The context of language*. Rowley, Massachusetts: Newbury House Publishers, 1976.

Wardhaugh, Ronald. Theories of language acquisition in relation to beginning reading instruction. *Language Learning,* 1971, *21,* 1-26.

Watts, A.F. *The language and mental development of children*. London: George G. Harrap, 1967.

Weir, Ruth H. *Language in the crib*. The Hague: Mouton, 1962.

Weisenburger, Janet L. A choice of words: Two year old speech from a situational point of view. *Journal of Child Language,* 1976, *3,* 275-281.

Wells, Gordon. Learning to code experience through language. *Journal of child Language,* 1974, *1,* 243-269.

Werner, Heinz, & Kaplan, Bernard. *The acquisition of word meaning: A developmental study.* Monographs of the Society for Research in Child Development #15, 1952.

Werner, Heinz, & Kaplan, Bernard. *Symbol formation.* New York: John Wiley and Sons, 1963.

White, Evelyn Mae. Linguistic learning cycles. *Reading Teacher,* 1968, *21,* 411-413.

White, Robert W. Motivation reconsidered: The concept of competence. *Psychological Review,* 1959, *66,* 297-333.

Whorf, Benjamin L. *Language, thought, and reality.* Cambridge, Masschusetts: MIT Press, 1956.

Williams, Frederick, & Naremore, Rita C. On the functional analysis of social class differences in modes of speech. *Speech Monographs,* 1969, *36,* 77-102.

Williams, Roger M. Why children should draw. *Saturday Review,* September 3, 1977, 11-15.

Willoughby, R.R. The functions of conversation. *Journal of Social Psychology,* 1932, *3,* 146-160.

Wilson, Stephen. The use of ethnographic techniques in educational research. *Review of Educational Research,* 1977, *47,* 245-265.

Wiseman, D. Spelling: The beginnings of literacy. *Reading Horizons,* 1980, *29,* 311-313.

Wolf, Robert L., & Rhodes, Gregory L. *Towards understanding naturalistic inquiry in educational research and evaluation.* Bloomington: Indiana University, 1977.

Wolf, Robert L., & Tymitz, Barbara. Ethnography and reading: Matching inquiry mode to process. *Reading Research Quarterly,* 1976-1977, **12,** 5-11.

Wolf, Robert L., & Tymitz, Barbara. Toward more natural inquiry in education. *Center on Evaluation, Development, and Research,* 1977, 1-4.

Wood, Barbara S. *Children and communication: Verbal and nonverbal language development.* Englewood Cliffs, New Jersey: Prentice-Hall, 1981.

Wright, Herbert F. Observational child study. In Paul H. Mussen (Ed.), *Handbook of research methods in child development.* New York: John Wiley and Sons, 1960, 71-139.

Wright, Herbert F. *Recording and analyzing child behavior.* New York: Harper and Row, 1967.

Yardley, Alice. *Exploration and language.* London: Evans Brothers, 1970.

Zaporozhets, A.V. The development of perception in the preschool child. In P. H. Mussen (Ed.), *European research in child development. Monographs of the Society for Research in Child Development,* 1965, *30,* 82-101.

Zaporozhets, A.V., & Elkonin, D.B. *The psychology of preschool children.* Cambridge, Massachusetts: MIT Press, 1971.

Zigler, Edward. The environment mystique: Training the intellect versus development of the child *Childhood Education,* 1970, *46,* 402-412.

Zutell, Jerry. Some psycholinguistic perspectives on children's spelling. *Language Arts,* 1978,*3 55,* 844-850.

Zyve, C.I. Conversation among children. *Teachers College Record,* 1927, *29,* 46-61.

Bibliography of Giti's Books

Barrett, Judi. *I Hate to Take a Bath*. New York: Four Winds Press, 1975.

Bemelmans, Ludwig. *Madeline*. New York: Puffin Books, 1967.

Berenstain, Stanley, & Berenstain, Janice. *The Berenstains' B Book*. New York: Random House, 1971.

Berenstain, Stanley, & Berenstain, Janice. *New Baby*. New York: Random House, 1974.

Brandenberg, Franz. *I Wish I Was Sick Too*. New York: Random House, 1976.

Brown, Margaret Wise. *The Runaway Bunny*. New York: Harper and Row, 1942.

Chamberlin, Mary Jo. *The Sleepy Puppy*. Racine, Wisconsin: A Whitman Book, 1956.

de Brunhoff, Laurent. *Babar Saves the Day*. New York: Random House, 1976.

de Brunhoff, Laurent. *Meet Babar and His Family*. New York: Random House, 1973.

Donald Duck: The Play Along Book. Racine, Wisconsin: Western Publishing, 1977.

Dunn, Judy. *The Little Duck*. New York: Random House, 1976.

Dunn, Judy. *The Little Lamb*. New York: Random House, 1977.

Eastman, P.D. *Big Dog, Little Dog*. New York: Random House, 1973.

Eastman, P.D. *Flap Your Wings*. New York: Random House, 1977.

Edwards, Zeny. *A Day at the Zoo*. New York: Prestige Books, 1976.

Farm Friends. Racine, Wisconsin: Western Publishing, 1971.

Federico, Helen. *A Golden Sturdy Book of Counting*. New York: Western Publishing, 1969.

Five Hundred Words to Grow On. New York: Random House, 1973.

Frank, Josette. *Poems to Read to the Very Young*. New York: Random House, 1977.

French, Laura. *Dinosaurs*. Racine, Wisconsin: Western Publishing, 1975.

Fulton, Janet. *The Raggedy Ann Book*. Racine, Wisconsin: Western Publishing, 1969.

Gergely, Tibor. *Busy Day, Busy People*. New York: Random House, 1973.

Hoban, Russell. *A Bargain for Frances*. New York: Scholastic Book Service, 1970.

Hogan, Cecily Ruth. *Lassie and Her Friends*. New York: Golden Press, 1975.

Hulick, Nancy. *Little Golden Picture Dictionary*. Racine, Wisconsin: Western Publishing, 1976.

Kent, Jack. Hop, Skip, and Jump Book. New York: Random House, 1974.

Kingsley, Emily Perl. *Big Bird and Little Bird's Big and Little Book*. Racine, Wisconsin: Western Publishing, 1977.

Krinsky, Jeanette. *Summer Friends*. New York: Wonder Books, 1976.

Kunhardt, Dorothy. *Pat the Bunny*. Racine, Wisconsin: Western Publishing, n.d.

Lippman, Peter. *Busy Wheels*. New York: Random House, 1973.

Little Red Riding Hood. Racine, Wisconsin: A Whitman Book, 1964.

Lööf, Jan. *Uncle Louie's Fantastic Sea Voyage*. New York: Random House, 1977.

Lööf, Jan. *Who's Got the Apple?* New York: Random House.

Mayer, Mercer. *Just For You*. New York: Golden Press, 1975.

McNaught, Harry. *Animal Babies*. New York: Random House, 1977.

Miller, Roberta. *Golden Counting Book*. Racine, Wisconsin: Western Publishing, 1962.

Milne, A.A. *When We Were Very Young*. New York: E.P. Dutton, 1924.

Mother Goose. New York: Randon House, 1973.

Mother Goose Book. New York: McGraw-Hill, 1960.

Moss, Jeffrey. *People in Your Neighborhood*. Children's Television Workshop, 1971.

Old Macdonald Had a Farm. Racine, Wisconsin: Western Publishing, 1960.

Pfloog, Jan. *Kittens Are Like That*. New York: Random House, 1976.

Pfloog, Jan. *Puppies Are Like That*. New York: Random House, 1975.

Potter, Beatrix. *The Tale of the Flopsy Bunnies*. New York: Frederick Warne, 1909.

Provensen, Alice & Provensen, Martin. *A Book of Seasons*. New York: Random House, 1976.

Provensen, Alice, & Provensen, Martin. *Old Mother Hubbard*. New York: Random House, 1977.

Provensen, Alice, & Provensen, Martin. *Roses Are Red. Are Violets Blue?* New York: Random House, 1973.

Raggedy Ann and Andy at the Zoo. New York: Bobbs-Merrill, 1974.

Raggedy Ann's Favorite Things. Racine, Wisconsin: Western Publishing, 1972.

Scarry, Richard. *Lowly Worm Storybook*. New York: Random House, 1977.

Scarry, Richard. *Please and Thank You Book*. New York: Random House, 1973.

Schobert, Geri. *Books Are Fun*. Racine, Wisconsin: Western Publishing, 1974.

Seuss, Dr. *Marvin K. Mooney, Will You Please Go Now!* New York: Random House, 1972.

Singer, Arthur. Wild Animals. New York: Random House, 1973.

Sleeping Beauty. New York: Random House, 1977.

Sonneborn, Ruth A. *Someone Is Eating the Sun*. New York: Random House, 1974.

Spinney, Caroll E. *How to Be a Grouch*. Racine, Wisconsin: Western Publishing, 1976.

Stevenson, Robert Louis. *A Child's Garden of Verses*. New York: Random House, 1978.

Stiles, Norman, & Wilcox, Daniel. *Grover and the Everything in the Whole Wide World Museum*. New York: Random House, 1974.

Stone, Jon. *Hide and Seek*. New York: Random House, 1976.

The Big Time Book. New York: Mulberry Books, n.d.

The Country Mouse and the City Mouse. New York: Random House, 1977.

The Mulberry Bush. Chicago: Rand McNally, 1969.

The Night Before Christmas. New York: Random House, 1975.

The Three Bears. Racine, Wisconsin: Western Publishing, 1973.

The Three Pigs. New York: Random House, 1973.

The Winnie-the Pooh Book. Racine, Wisconsin: Western Publishing, 1965.

Three Little Kittens. New York: Random House, 1974.

Three Little Pigs. New York: Random House, 1977.

Vasiliu, Mircea. *A Day at the Beach*. New York: Random House, 1977.

Watson, Jane Werner. *Birds*. Racine, Wisconsin: Western Publishing, 1958.

Winnie-the-Pooh and His Friends. Racine, Wisconsin: Western Publishing, 1976.

Zallinger, Peter. *Dinosaurs*. New York: Random House, 1977.

Appendix 1
Procedure Summary

Choice of Method:	Case Study
Subject:	Daughter:
Time Line:	Birth to three years of age
Participant Observer:	Mother
Third Person Observers:	Father, grandparents, family friends

RECORD-KEEPING

Daily:	sample tape recording of oral language
	transcriptions of context for dialogue between mother and child
	log of time spent in parent-child interaction
	folder of writing and drawing samples
Monthly:	half hour videotape encounter with print
	one hour cassette of oral language
Longitudinally:	diary of experiences and activities
	notebook of observations, speculations
	description of the home environment
	cataloging of books, play equipment
	notations of reading interests

ANALYSIS

Longitudinal:	draw parallels between language acquisition and learning to read
Qualitative:	delineate functions for which child uses linguistic strategies with print

Appendix 2
Diagram of Giti's Room

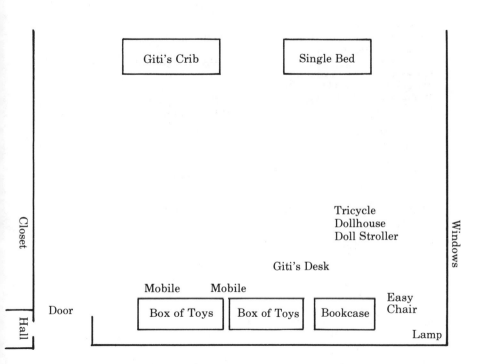

Appendix 3
Early Reading Interactions

24 Months

Mother	Giti
Here's a book. Can you read that? That's one of your nice books. Can you read that?	Lassie [onamadawe]. (She pushes *Lassie and Her Friends* at me.)
Shall we read it together? What's the name of it. O.K. Lassie and Her Friends. It's called *Lassie and Her Friends.* Lassie is a wise and gentle collie dog. She is a special friend of all the animal babies on the farm.	[dashar]. Lassie [afriyn]. [dis] is called. Farm. (She hits the picture of a butterfly.)
What's that?	A butterfly.
A butterfly. Um hum. Good.	
Lassie watches the lambs as they frisk about on the grass.	Lassie grass.
O.K. What's this say?	You read.
When the cat plays, Lassie plays too.	Fur. Soft. Too.
What's this one?	Kitty.
Lassie likes to run with the little foal. See how they chase each other in the meadow.	See [dow].
O.K. What are those? Yeah, the pigs are all dirty.	Pigs are dirty.
Lassie isn't going to play with the baby pigs today. The pigs are all dirty from rolling around in the mud.	
In the woods, Lassie finds a baby chipmunk and a bunny.	Baby chipmunk. A bunny.
Where's the bunny?	It's here. (She points.)
Lassie looks up in the trees. Mother Squirrel is chattering to her babies.	
O.K. What's happening here?	The duck.
The duck. O.K.	
Sometimes Lassie swims in the pond. Don't worry, Mother Duck, Lassie won't hurt your babies.	
	Lassie. Goat.
Yea. A goat and lassie.	
Watch out Lassie, those silly little goats play too hard.	Goats. Too hard.

Fuzzy chicks are funny to watch as they peck peck on the ground. (Mother demonstrates pecking with her forefinger.) Peck. Yea, like that. Peck, Peck. They're eating.

Peck.

Mother cat knows that Lassie is her friend. Lassie licks the soft, mewing kittens.

Cat.
[friyn]

Lassie is a good friend of boys and girls too. It's fun to play with Lassie. O.K.

Mother	Giti
Do you want to read this one by yourself?	No, no. (She pushes *Summer Friends* at me to read.)
Let's read it together. *Summer Friends.* This one is called *Summer Friends.*	
At the end of the summer, Susie's said, "Tomorrow we are going back home to the city."	At end. Tomorrow we home city. (She echoes while I read.)
So Susie went to say goodbye to all her summer friends.	[friyns]
Good.	
She went to the meadow. "Goodbye Mr. Grasshopper, " she said.	Grasshopper.
"Would you like to come to the city with me?	Oh no.
"Oh no," said the grasshopper. "I couldn't jump in the city streets."	
She went to the cow. "Goodbye, Mrs. Cow. Would like to come to the city with me?	Oh no.
"Oh no. You don't have such green grass in the city."	Oh no. You have green grass city. (She echoes while I read.)
She went to the ducks "Hello, little ducks. Would you like to come to the city with me?"	Went to the ducks. Oh no.
"Oh no," said the ducks, "We couldn't come to the city with you. We live in the pond."	
She went to the frog. She went to the bunny rabbit.	Frog. Bunny rabbit. She went to the frog.
She went to the birds. She went to the flowers.	The birds.
But no one, not even one, would go to the city with Susie. Susie felt very sad. She thought and thought and then she knew what she would do.	

What would she do? Let's turn the
page.

With her big box of crayons on a big white paper, she drew her summer friends.	Paper.
She drew the grasshopper. She drew the frog. She drew the ducks. She drew the bunny. She drew the birds.	Susie drawing.
That's Susie drawing.	Susie drawing.
Here's the picture that Susie drew. And there's everything. Susie's drawing. Is Susie happy?	Susie happy.

Good.

How about your book about Winnie-the-Pooh? Do you think you can read this yourself?	No, Mommy. You. You.
O.K. Let's try this book.	
Who's this book about?	Winnie Pooh.
Right.	
Winnie-the-Pooh lives in a house in the forest. Here is Pooh Bear with his friend Christopher Robin. They are reading a funny story.	Pooh Bear. Story.
Um hum.	
Shy Piglet is afraid of his own shadow. There's nothing Pooh likes better than eating honey with piglet.	
Where's the honey?	(She points to the honey pot.) Honey.
Who's this?	Tiger.
Right, Tigger is Pooh's bouncy friend. And owl is Pooh's knowing friend. He explains things to Pooh.	E-ore. E-ore.
Right. Eyeore is a gloomy friend. He's a donkey, see?	Donkey.
Now Eyeore is happy. He's glad to see Winnie-the-Pooh. Winnie-the-Pooh is happy to see Eyeore.	Winnie Pooh happy. Susie happy. Lassie happy. Mommy happy. Baba happy.
Sometimes Pooh has tea at rabbit's house.	Teapot.
Now Pooh is visiting Kanga and Baby Roo. Sometimes Roo rides in Kanga's pocket.	
Pooh has a lot of friends and here they are all together.	[dey] are.
O.K.	

26 Months

Mother	Giti
Can you read this book for me? *(Old Macdonald Had a Farm.)*	eieieiei. eieieiei.
Good.	eieieieieieie.
That's O.K.	eieieieieie.
What is this?	He had some chicks.
Yeah.	Chick chack here chick. eieieieieieiei.
	He had some pigs. eieieieieiei.
What are these?	Ducks.
What do ducks do?	Kack, kack. eieieiei.
What are these?	Here? Hum.
Are they turkeys?	Turkeys. Yeah.
What do turkeys do?	Kack, kack, kack. Gobble, gobble, gobble. eieieieieiei.
Good.	
	Oink, oink, oink, here.
Oink, oink.	Kack, here.
What are these?	Moooooo.
	They have bells.
Where are bells? Show me the bells.	They have bells on their neck.
Right. Oh wow.	Moooo. eieieieiei.
O.K.	
What are they doing?	Hee haw, hee haw.
Hee haw.	eieieieiei go hee haw.
What are these?	Baa, baa, baa.
Baa. That's right. They're sheep.	Hay.
Hay, right. Near the barn.	
What are these?	They have apple on the tree.
Yeah, apples on the tree.	They eating the apple.
Yeah, apples on the tree.	They eating the apple.

Mother	Giti
Can you read this book for Mommy?	The Third Bears kind.
Yeah, The Three Bears. That's the kind.	
O.K. There's a baba bear, momma bear, and a baby bear.	Momma Bear is making a big cake for the three bears. Coming.
	Oh no, you read.

Not far away a little golden haired girl was picking berries in the forest. (Let's look at the book.) The girl's name is Goldilocks and as she picked berries, her button nose went sniff, sniff.

Sniff, sniff. (She demonstrates.)

"Porridge," said Goldilocks, "Smells good," and she followed her nose. Goldilocks came to the three bears' house and saw that the door was open. She peeked inside and saw the three bowls of porridge. "Oh my," she said.

Oh my.

Goldilocks tasted some porridge from Papa Bear's big bowl. It was too hot, and the porridge in Mama Bear's medium sized bowl was too cold, but the porridge in Baby Bear's little bowl was just right and Goldilocks ate it all up.

Here she is rubbing her tummy.

With a tummy full of warm porridge, Goldilocks looked into the livingroom and saw three chairs. She tried Papa Bear's great big chair, but it was too hard, and Mama Bear's medium chair, but it was too soft, and Baby Bear's little chair looked just right, but, when she sat down, "Crunch."

The chair broke.

Right, the chair broke. Goldilocks went upstairs and saw three beds. She tried Papa Bear's great big bed, but it was too hard, and Mama Bear's medium sized bed was too soft. But Baby Bear's bed was just right and when Goldilocks lay down in it, she fell asleep.

Hard.

The three bears got back from their walk and Paper Bear growled, "Who forgot to close the door?" and Mama Bear said, "You forgot to close the door." and Baby Bear squeaked, "Who me?"

Who forgot to close the door? (She echoes in an exaggerated voice.) You forgot to close the door.
Who me? Who me? Who me?

Inside, Papa Bear growled "Somebody's been eating my porridge." "Somebody's been eating my porridge," said Mama Bear." "Somebody's been eating my porridge," squeaked Baby Bear, "and they ate it all up."

Ate it all up.

Baghban

From the living room, Papa Bear growled, "Somebody's been sitting in my chair." "And somebody's been sitting in my chair," said Mama Bear. "And somebody's been sitting in my chair, too," squeaked Baby Bear, "And they broke it."

One by one the three bears went up the stairs and Papa Bear growled, "Somebody's been sleeping in my bed." "And somebody's been sleeping in my bed," said Mama Bear. But Baby Bear didn't say a thing. He just looked at the bed. Papa Bear growled, "What's this?" "What's this?" asked Mama Bear.

In my bed.

What's this?

"Somebody's been sleeping in my bed, too and she still is," squeaked Baby Bear. "It's a little girl."

Goldilocks opened her eyes and looked at the three bears. The three bears looked at Goldilocks. "I-I-I'm sorry," said Goldilocks and she jumped up and ran down the stairs and out of the house as fast as she could go. "Next time," growled Papa Bear, "That little girl will remember her manners." Mama Bear said, "There's still plenty of porridge for our breakfast." "I hope she can come to visit us again," squeaked Baby Bear. "She seemed very nice."

And that's the story of the three bears. O.K.

30 Months

Mother	Giti
Let's read one of your books. How about this one? You were going to read this one in the car this morning. Remember, *Big Bird and Little Bird*. You want to put it there? (She motions to the table.) O.K. you just hold it flat on your lap.	Big Bird and Little Bird. (She reads the cover.) Big Bird and Little Bird. (She reads the title page.) Big Bird and Little Bird. (She reads the first page.)
Yeah.	
What's this say?	I love balloons.
Good.	I love fountains.

Un huh.	I love whales.
Keep reading.	I love big boats.
What happens after that?	I love big mountains.
Ohhhh.	I like to feed the hippopotamus.
	See the balloon. (She points.)
Um hum.	
Good. It's flying in the air.	
Ohhh.	I like to feed the bunny.
	Who's that?
Isn't that Grover?	Grover.
	What's that?
I don't know. Another muppet.	It's a man.
A man. O.K.	
	Oh, what's that?
	Oh, what's that, Mommy? (Louder)
A baton.	A baton.
Um hum.	
What's this one?	Accordion.
Good. Tuba.	Tuba.
Do yoy know this word?	[sese] you. (Sesame Street)
O.K. Let's turn the page. You read it. You're almost finished.	You read it. I cannot read it.
You read it all the time.	
O.K. I'll finish it.	
I like a great big long freight train. And what does he like?	Freight train.
His little electric train.	Electric train.
What's this over here? (She points.)	Tunnel.
Right, tunnel. O.K. What's this? (She points.)	Tunnel.
This one right here over the water.	Tun-nel.
O.K. that's a bridge over the water.	Bridge.
My favorite dog is a great dane.	Dane.
My favorite dog is a Chihuahua. Good	(She points.) Chihuahua.
Who's this in the can?	It's Grouch in the can.
It's Grouch.	
Who's this one?	Ernie's there.
Ernie's there.	

Who's this?	Bert.
Bert.	
O.K. Who's this holding the dog?	It's Buffie.
It's Big Bird but he's not standing up straight. He looks different. Here's Big Bird and that's Little Bird. Now where are they?	[dis] Big Bird and Little Bird.
O.K. There Little Bird.	
	What's that?
That's a trapeze artist.	
	There's Ernie.
Yeah.	
	I want the...oh-oh...
Um hum.	Look at [dis].
	What's that?
That's Bert and Ernie. They're in the audience.	Bert.
O.K. At the circus, what does Big Bird like? At the circus he says, "I like the elephants." At the circus, Little Bird says, "I like the trained fleas." O.K.	
Now what does he like. I like... Watermelon.	Watermelon.
What does Little Bird like?	
He likes grapes.	
You know, Little Bird, even though I like all those great big things, I can think of one little thing I like a whole lot.	
Really, I can think of one big thing that I really like too.	YOU.
You.	
Good girl. We finished your book.	

Appendix 4
Signs Giti Read at 26 Months

Ayr-Way	Eisner
Kmart	Osco
Krogers	7-Up
McDonalds	7 Eleven
Stop	Railroad Crossing
Sears	Cheerios
Rice Krispies	Arbys
Burger King	Marsh
Wendys	Big Wheel
Dairy Queen	A & W
Sambos	I G A

Appendix 5
Self-Motivated Selections of Books for One Month
(at age 30 months)

Title of Book	Person Reading			Date
	Mother	Father	Self	
Roses Are Red, Are Violets Blue?	x			
Summer Friends				
People in Your Neighborhood			x	2/1
Flopsy Bunnies		x		
Wild Animals	x		x	
500 Words to Grow On	x		x	2/2
Busy Day, Busy People	x		x	
Dinosaurs		x		
Raggedy Ann and Andy at the Zoo	x		x x	
New Baby			x	
Winnie-the-Pooh and His Friends	x			
Donald Duck	x			
Farm Friends	x			
Her Name Book		x		2/3
Raggedy Ann and Andy at the Zoo			x	
New Baby			x	
Pat the Bunny			x	
Big and Little Book			x	

Title					Date
Grover and the Whole Wide World			x		
Pat the Bunny			x x x		2/4
Birds			x		
New Baby			x		
Busy Wheels	x				
Busy Day, Busy People	x				
Raggedy Ann and Andy at the Zoo			x		
Roses Are Red, Are Violets Blue?			x		
Donald Duck			x		
Mother Goose	x		x		
Pat the Bunny			x		
Donald Duck				x	2/5
Mother Goose			x		
Three Little Kittens	xxx	xx			
Who's Got the Apple?	xx		xx		
Mulberry Bush	x		xxx		
Birds	x		x		
Who's Got the Apple?	x				
Three Little Kittens	x		x		
Mulberry Bush			xx		2/6
Birds			x		
Bill Bunny's Surprise	x	x	x		
Busy Wheels			xx		
Bill Bunny's Surprise	x		x		
Mulberry Bush			x		2/7
Busy Wheels			x		
How to Be a Grouch	x				
Counting	x				
A Child's Garden of Verses	x				
Who's Got the Apple?		x			
Little Golden Picture Dictionary			x		2/8
Hop, Skip, and Jump Book			x		
Alphabet Book			x		
Who's Got the Apple?	x				
Donald Duck			x		2/9
Birds	x		x		
Three Little Kittens	x				
Raggedy Ann Book			x		
The Three Pigs			x		
New Baby			x		
Farm Friends	x				2/10
Wild Animals			x		

Title				
The Winnie-the-Pooh Book	x			
Wild Animals	x			
Grover and the Whole Wide World			x	
Mulberry Bush			x	2/11
Mother Goose	x			
Dinosaurs	x			
The Three Bears	x			
Old Macdonald Had a Farm	x			
Old Macdonald Had a Farm			xxx	
Donald Duck			x	
The Three Bears	x			
When We Were Very Young	x		xxx	
Busy Day, Busy People			x	
When We Were Very Young			xxx	
Old Macdonald Had a Farm			xxxx	
Roses Are Red, Are Violets Blue?	x			
The Three Little Pigs	x			
A Day at the Zoo	x			2/13
Raggedy Ann's Favorite Things			x	
Summer Friends			x	
One Little Indian		x		
People in Your Neighborhood	x		x	
Mulberry Bush	x		xxx	
People in Your Neighborhood			x	
Three Little Kittens			x	2/14
Mother Goose	x		x	
New Baby		x	x	
Flopsy Bunnies	x			
Sleepy Puppy	x			
Little Red Riding Hood	x			2/15
Donald Duck	x			
Farm Friends	x			
Little Red Riding Hood	x			
Pat the Bunny	x		x	
A Day at the Zoo	x			
Raggedy Ann and Andy at the Zoo	x			
Counting	x			2/16
Simple Objects (red)	x		x	
Simple Objects (green)	x		x	
Wild Animals	x		x	
The Big Time Book		x		
People in Your Neighborhood	x		xx	
500 Words to Grow On	x			
Big Dog, Little Dog	x			
Mulberry Bush	x		xx	
Hop, Skip, and Jump Book			x	

Hop, Skip, and Jump Book	x				
People in Your Neighborhood			x		2/17
Big Dog, Little Dog	x				
500 Words to Grow On			x		
Books Are Fun			x		2/18
Hop, Skip, and Jump Book			x		
Busy Wheels		x			
A Child's Garden of Verses		x			
A Child's Garden of Verses	x		x		
Busy Wheels	x				
Sleepy Puppy			x		
Flopsy Bunnies			x		
Counting			x		2/19
Summer Friends			x		
Big and Little Book			xx		
500 Words to Grow On				x	
Who's Got the Apple?	x				
Birds			x		
Three Little Kittens	x				
Roses Are Red, Are Violets Blue?	x				
Big and Little Book			x		
Hop, Skip, and Jump Book			x		2/20
Donald Duck			x		
Farm Friends			x		
500 Words to Grow On	x				
People in Your Neighborhood	x				
The Winnie-the-Pooh Book	x				
Mother Goose		x			
The Runaway Bunny	x	x			
Hop, Skip, and Jump Book			xxx		
500 Words to Grow On	x				
Runaway Bunny	x		x		2/21
A Day at the Zoo			x		
New Baby	x				
Busy Day, Busy People	x				
The Three Bears	x		x		
Hop, Skip, and Jump Book	x	x	x		2/22
New Baby	x		x		
Hop, Skip, and Jump Book			x		
Busy Day, Busy People	x				
Mulberry Bush			xxx		2/23
Old Macdonald Had a Farm	x		x		
Counting			x		
Runaway Bunny	x				
People in Your Neighborhood			x		
Farm Friends			x		
Little Golden Picture Dictionary	x		x		

Dinosaurs	x			
One Little Indian	x			
Little Golden Picture Dictionary			x	2/24
Sleepy Puppy	x		x	
Wild Animals			x	
The Winnie-the-Pooh Book	x			
Hop, Skip, and Jump Book			x	
Counting			x	
Mother Goose	x			
Hop, Skip, and Jump Book			x	
The Big Time Book		x		2/25
Lassie and Her Friends	x			
Who's Got the Apple?	x			
Puppies Are Like That		x		
Winnie-the-Pooh and His Friends	xx			
Books Are Fun			x	
Mulberry Bush			xxxx	
The Raggedy Ann Book		x		2/26
New Baby		x		
Who's Got the Apple?	x			
500 Words to Grow On			x	
Counting			x	
Old Macdonald Had a Farm	xx		xx	
Little Golden Picture Dictionary			x	
Little Red Riding Hood	x			
The Raggedy Ann Book	x			2/27
Lassie and Her Friends			x	
When We Were Very Young	x			
Pat the Bunny			x	
Big and Little Book			x	
Busy Day, Busy People	x			
Three Little Kittens	x			
Three Little Pigs		x		
Old Macdonald Had a Farm			x	
Little Golden Picture Dictionary			x	2/28
Three Little Kittens			x	

A Personal Note from the Author

This case study on our daughter's acquisition of oral language, reading, and writing began in 1976 while I was a doctoral student at Indiana University. Throughout my research I noted an increase in qualitative studies in education, and was impressed by the common themes, "Why do most children learn to talk, but not all children learn to read and write?" and "Why do so many children dislike reading and writing?" It seemed logical to me to investigate these issues as early as possible in the life of a single child. Observing our daughter, Giti, provided this opportunity. The original study covers the first three years of her life. This updated version includes information from three to five years of age.

I would like to thank Pi Lambda Theta Honor Society in Education and the Indiana University Dissertation Grants-in-Aid for providing the financial assistance which allowed the purchase of quality sound cassettes and videotapes to record the research data for my dissertation. I would also like to express my appreciation to my doctoral committee: Anabel Newman, Jerome Harste, Carolyn Burke, and Beverly Hartford, to Linda Prince for the original typing of the dissertation at Indiana University, and to Toby Muncy for typing the revised version at the College of Graduate Studies.

I would like to thank my parents, Mr. and Mrs. Frederick Moses, who have supported my education throughout my life. Their visits, when they assumed responsibility for Giti's care, provided me with time to write.

This study involved a total family context. My husband, Hafiz, also read to Giti, wrote notes to her, pointed out signs, took her to the library, and received her drawings and notes. For his support, both as a participant observer and as an editor, I would like to express my love and appreciation.

In Afghan folklore, it is believed that King Solomon, as ruler of both human and animal kingdoms, could communicate with animals. One tale begins with his asking the rabbit to search out the most beautiful baby in the world. The rabbit looks and looks everywhere. Finally, she returns with her own bunny and says, "Look how beautiful she is! Have you ever seen such bright eyes? See what fuzzy, soft hair she has." To my own baby bunny for her uniqueness and her existence, I am forever grateful. I can only hope that in her adult life she will see this work as a gift from me to her.

MB

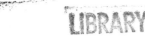